GROWING PLANS

GROWING PLANS

LYLE E. SCHALLER

Illustrated by EDWARD LEE TUCKER

Abingdon Press
Nashville

GROWING PLANS

Library of Congress Cataloging in Publication Data

SCHALLER, LYLE E.
Growing plans.
Includes bibliographical references.
1. Church growth. I. Title.
BV652.25.S34   1983   254'5   82-16330

ISBN 0-687-15962-8

MANUFACTURED BY THE PARTHENON PRESS AT
NASHVILLE, TENNESSEE, UNITED STATES OF AMERICA

To
Albert H. Buhl,
Erston M. Butterfield,
and
Otto W. Toelke

CONTENTS

INTRODUCTION

The twenty-five-year history of the Church Growth Movement has produced scores, perhaps even hundreds, of different models and strategies for evangelism. This book does *not* represent an attempt to review, summarize, or evaluate that growing body of church growth models. That task must be left to a more ambitious analyst with another set of goals.

Despite this plethora of creative ideas and programs, the best single approach still is the old-fashioned system of personal visitation. This system affirms the value of face-to-face relationships and requires the pastor and lay volunteers to call, on a regular basis, on individuals and families who do not have an active relationship with any worshiping congregation. Some experienced practitioners of this approach contend that a *minimum* of six visits must be made, perhaps a month or two apart, before any decision can be made on whether or not that person's name should be retained on the list of prospective new members. Experience suggests that ten thousand such calls, some made by the pastor and others by carefully trained lay people, will result in one hundred to two hundred new members' uniting with the congregation. If all of the calling is done by the pastor and/or a trained lay parish visitor and is directed at the first residents of new single-family homes, the response rate may be a little higher. If the calling is done entirely by laity who do not live in the community where the church building is, and if there are significant language, racial, or socio-economic class differences between the callers and the persons visited, the response rate may be somewhat lower.

This endorsement of visitation evangelism is offered partly to affirm that approach, but primarily to introduce the first of the seven basic assumptions on which this book is based. The first assumption is that there are some congregations that cannot enlist the necessary number of volunteers who possess the appropriate gifts and commitment for this approach to evangelism. This shortage tends to be especially prevalent among long-established congregations in which most of the people who might volunteer for this approach have been members of the congregation for at least a dozen years, and there has been a change of pastors since they united with that church. The most effective lay volunteers for visitation evangelism come in disproportionately large numbers from among those who have been members for less than three years, and who have joined since the arrival of the present minister.

A corollary to this first assumption, and one that many lay readers may find difficult to accept, is that there are some pastors who are very interested in church growth, but who are less than enthusiastic about visitation evangelism.

The last comment on visitation evangelism is that, despite the basic value of the approach, there are many congregations for which it is not the appropriate strategy.

The second major assumption on which this book is based is that no two congregations are identical, and the most significant single factor in identifying the differences among congregations is size.[1] That assumption is the primary reason for suggesting that (a) every congregation would be well advised to tailor its church growth strategy to maximize its resources, assets, and strengths, including the unique gifts and talents of its pastor, and (b) a strategy that may be effective for one size church may not be appropriate for a different size congregation. The bulk of this book is devoted to describing three different strategies, one for small-membership churches, one for middle-sized congregations, and one for large churches.

The third assumption is one that should not need to be defended, but thousands of congregations appear not to believe it: No congregation exists in complete isolation from all other churches. The fact that that assumption is not universally accepted is a major theme in the epistles of Paul. The reality of this assumption, however, should be apparent to every denominationally related congregation on the North American continent. The actions, policies, publications, guidelines, and priorities of the denomination affect the evangelistic outreach of every congregation in the denominational family. This is most apparent, of course, in the more "connectional" denominations; such as Anglican,

Methodist, Presbyterian, Episcopal, Catholic, and since 1962 or 1969, the three largest Lutheran bodies.

This third assumption provides the rationale for including in a brief last chapter several short comments about the formulation of a denominational strategy for church growth.

The policies, programs, and priorities of the denomination in the allocation of financial resources, in ministerial placement, in new church development, in the priorities placed on the time and energy of denominational staff, in the content of denominational periodicals, in the expectations placed on pastors and congregations, in the curriculum in the theological seminaries, in the emphasis placed on evangelism, and the components of that denominational strategy for church growth will affect the evangelistic outreach of most congregations in the denominational family.

The fourth assumption is based on two generalizations. First, church growth strategies in long-established congregations tend to be most effective in attracting people with an active church relationship. The long-established churches tend to be heavily involved in a game that has been described as "the circulation of the saints."[2] By contrast, the Lutheran Church in America, the Reformed Church in America, the Southern Baptist Convention, the Baptist General Conference, and a score of other smaller denominations have demonstrated that it is possible to develop a model for new church development in which two-thirds to four-fifths of the members of a new mission will be adults who, previous to joining that new congregation, were not active in the life of any worshiping congregation.

12

In the formulation of a denominational strategy for reaching the unchurched, the organization of new congregations should be the number-one priority, but only one component of such a strategy. Therefore, a brief chapter is included in this volume that raises and discusses some of the issues that are a part of the process of formulating a denominational strategy for new church development.

A fifth assumption that informs this book (but is especially influential in the last three chapters) is drawn from the economist's perspective on financial subsidies. In general, that which is subsidized increases in number, that which is taxed decreases in number. An example of this is the denominational policy that expects large congregations to subsidize small-membership churches. The predictable response is an increase in the number of small-membership churches and a decrease in the number of large congregations. The position taken in this book is that *long-term* denominational financial subsidies weaken new missions and churches of all sizes.

Sixth, every approach to church growth rests on a foundation of values, goals, dreams, prejudices, assumptions, interpretations of reality, theological perspectives, and understandings of the biblical imperative.

A basic assumption on which this book rests has three facets: (a) it is good for individual Christians to be a part of a worshiping congregation—the hermit Christian is a contradiction in terms, (b) it is good for congregations to receive new members into their fellowship—they enrich the life and ministry of that congregation,[3] and (c) denominations tend to be healthier, to place a greater emphasis on mission and ministry, to be more open to new ideas, to be more responsive to change, and to be less oriented toward institutional survival goals when they are experiencing numerical growth. New members bring a breath of fresh air to congregations and to denominational gatherings. In brief, not only is there no automatic conflict between numerical growth and faithfulness and obedience to the claims of the gospel, but numerical growth and faithfulness tend to go together. Numerical decline and a subversion of the goals of the churches also tend to go hand-in-hand in both congregations and denominational agencies.

Finally, I assume that every reader will disagree with some of the statements made in this book. That is normal and predictable behavior. It also is good! Some will disagree with a specific assumption or statement. Others will disagree with the general approach offered in one or more chapters. When that happens, it suggests a thoughtful reader has encountered a provocative sentence. The intent here is to be provocative, not definitive, in the discussion of various strategies.

These are some of the major assumptions that the five strategies suggested in this book are based on. For those who want to pursue the question of assumptions first, a dozen other assumptions about church growth are presented in the final chapter.

1

How Do Small Churches Grow?

"Most of our members would like to see our congregation grow in size, but they don't want to lose any of the intimacy, the close fellowship, the friendliness, or the sense of caring that distinguish our church," observed Harold Pierce, the minister of the 106-member Faith Church. Harold was in his seventh year at Faith Church. He also served a forty-member congregation that met in a small white frame building seven miles out in the country. His main concern, however, was many of the Faith Church members' desire to see their congregation grow, and their frustration with having no net increase in size.

During the past seven years Faith Church had lost nine members through death, eighteen through transfer of their membership to churches in other communities. (Eight of these were young adults who had grown up in Faith Church and moved away, while six others had moved to the Sunbelt to retire, ` and four had married into other denominations and had joined another church to be with their spouses.) Six other names had been removed from the membership roll by action of the governing board. These thirty-three losses had been offset by the addition of thirty-four new members, an average of five a year, but a net gain of only one in seven years.

"The folks out in the country church don't expect that church to grow, and they're quite content with things just the way they are. Many of the people here at Faith Church, however, believe this congregation should grow. They know there has been a seventeen percent increase in the population in our community since 1970, and they wonder why our church has almost exactly the same number of members we had back in 1970, or even back as far as 1950. For thirty-five years our membership has ranged between a low of 99 and a high of 114. They're the ones who sent me to this church growth workshop to find out what's wrong," concluded Harold. "How does a small congregation like Faith Church grow?"

There are at least eight responses that can be offered to Harold Pierce and to others concerned about the numerical growth of small-membership churches.

1. Rarely.
2. Reluctantly.
3. Only by accepting significant changes.
4. By several members' committing themselves to an "adopt-a-member" strategy. In this approach, a dozen or more members commit themselves to go out and to win a new member to the congregation and to help that new member gain a sense of belonging.[1]
5. By finding themselves surrounded by a flood

of newcomers to the community who come in, largely on their own initiative, and "take over" control of that long-established and stable small church. The newcomers change the style of congregational life to make numerical growth a real possibility.

6. By attracting a disproportionately large number of that three percent of the church population who move into a community, begin attending a nearby church, unite with that congregation, become hard workers in that church, move into leadership roles, and soon are widely regarded as beloved and influential leaders—and there is not much anyone can do to keep those self-starters out. The major disadvantage with this response is that self-starters are comparatively rare.

7. By a two-part program in which a group of leaders first commit themselves to a serious study of the Bible, with special emphasis on evangelism and the New Testament definition of the church. (The Word and Witness program of the Lutheran Church in America is an excellent example of this approach to Bible study.) The second part of the study program provides an opportunity for these leaders to participate in church growth workshops that provide both the inspiration and the "how-to" skills necessary for formulating and implementing a church growth strategy tailored to their congregation and the community in which the members live.

8. A "Pastor and Allies" strategy that places the responsibility for the primary initiative for a church growth program on the minister, and usually requires *at least* a five- or six-year pastorate to implement completely.

Before examining this last alternative in more

detail, it may be useful to explain why the first several answers to Harold Pierce's question appear to be so discouraging.

Why Don't Small Congregations Grow?

One fourth of all Protestant congregations on the North American continent average fewer than thirty-five at the Sunday morning worship service. At least one-half average less than seventy-five. Those two statements, while they startle many people, do represent reality. They suggest that the normative size for a Protestant congregation in the North American culture probably varies between twenty and sixty at the principal weekly worship service. One third of all Protestant congregations fit into this bracket.

There has been speculation about why that pattern is so prevalent. Perhaps the "natural" size of a congregation is what is usually identified as a "small church." Perhaps it is because the typical small church is not organized to grow, but is organized to remain on a plateau in size.[2] There also is a growing body of evidence that (a) long-established small-membership churches are often "lay owned and operated," rather than minister-centered, and (b) the greater the lay control in any size congregation, the less likely it is that the congregation will begin and maintain significant numerical growth. This runs counter to conventional ministerial wisdom, but is an accepted fact of life to most lay persons.

Others suggest that the primary reason the small-membership church tends not to grow is because it is too inward-oriented and most of the limited resources are concentrated on serving the members and on institutional survival. The small church tends to focus on nurture, not mission. Members of the small congregation also often assume that they do not possess the discretionary resources necessary to plan and implement a growth strategy. Several people also have observed that many of the most important symbols in the small church remind one of local events and traditions, not of the historic teachings of the Christian faith. Memorial plaques are one example.

One of the most frequently overlooked factors inhibiting the numerical growth of most small-membership churches is the age of that institution. There is a definite correlation between the age of a congregation and the probability of numerical growth. Today, numerically growing churches come in disproportionately large numbers from those congregations that have not yet reached their fifteenth birthday, and in disproportionately small numbers from the churches that have been in existence for several decades. Most small-membership churches have been in existence for three or more decades.

The length of the pastorate is also a factor. While there is no evidence to prove that long pastorates produce numerical growth, it is rare to find a congregation that has experienced and sustained a significant numerical growth without the benefit of a long pastorate. Relatively few small-membership churches have the leadership of the same pastor for more than three or four years.

Another explanation is that all of us excel in those areas of life in which we have had considerable practice and experience. The typical thousand-member congregation must receive an average of two new members a week to remain on a plateau in size. That means the large church has to practice enlisting and assimilating eight to ten new members every month. The eighty-member congregation may have to receive only three to five members a year in order to remain on a plateau in size—and three of the five are children born into the congregation, while a fourth married into it. As a result, the members in the small congregation have had very little practice or experience in recruiting and assimilating new members who do not have kinfolk in the congregation.

While it is seldom mentioned, a very significant factor behind the lack of numerical growth in many small congregations (especially among those urban churches that today are only a fraction of the size they were back in the 1950s or 1960s) is the low level of corporate self-esteem among the members. Frequently the members of these congregations see themselves as small, weak, unattractive, powerless, and frustrated with a limited future. That self-image often creates a self-perpetuating cycle that produces policies and decisions that inhibit the potential outreach. Their priorities are survival and institutional maintenance, not evangelism.

Perhaps the most persuasive single explanation of why small-membership churches tend to remain on a plateau in size or decline slowly, rather than to grow in numbers, is based on the theory of group life. The typical small-membership church often resembles an overgrown small group. The face-to-face contact of the members with one another, rather than shared institutional goals, a well-managed organizational structure, or an extensive program, is what draws and holds the people together. There is an obvious limit on the number of people who can be included, and feel included, in any such group. Since most of the members place a high value on the quality and depth of the interpersonal relationships in this size congregation, it is unreasonable to expect them to deliberately make the changes that will erode the advantages of these face-to-face relationships. Whom would you prefer to see elected to serve on the church council? A member you know only by reputation? Or someone who is a close friend, a relative, or a fellow member of the one adult Sunday school class?

Before moving on to the next point, notice must be taken of those who allege that the primary reason any congregation fails to grow, regardless of size, is the lack of Christian commitment among the members. That is nonsense! After interviewing lay persons from over five thousand congregations, including hundreds of leaders from small churches, I have found no evidence to suggest that the commitment to Jesus Christ as Lord and Savior is any less among the members of the small-membership churches than it is among the members of rapidly growing churches. There may be some differences in how members of different churches *express* their Christian commitment, but that is a different subject from the *depth* of commitment. Some Christians express their commitment by teaching in the Sunday school or serving on committees, others by visiting the sick and the lonely, a small percentage by regularly calling on the unchurched, and many by trying to live their convictions in and through their vocations. How Christians respond to the love of Jesus Christ may influence the potential for numerical growth, but that is primarily related to the differences in gifts, talents, personalities, and theological stance. It should not be seen as a measure of the depth of commitment of the individual members!

Assumptions Behind a Strategy for the New Minister

The "pastor plus allies" strategy suggested here is based on four critical assumptions that are derived from the group-life theory of why small churches tend to remain on a plateau in size. The first assumption is that, for the typical small-membership church to experience any sustained numerical growth, it must be transformed from what Carl Dudley describes as a "single cell" congregation,[3] or an overgrown small group, into a congregation of groups, classes, choirs, circles, and organizations. The best means of accomplishing this is NOT to attempt to divide that single central cell, but rather to create new groups or cells. Therefore an important foundation stone for the strategy described here is derived from research on planned change. Whenever possible, it usually is wiser to produce change by addition rather than by division or subtraction.[4]

The second assumption is that the initiative for such radical changes is unlikely to come from anyone within the membership. "If I had wanted to be a member of a big church, I would have joined a big church. The reason I'm a member here is that I prefer the values of the small church." This frequently heard statement explains why most new members will not initiate a strategy to turn the small-membership church into a large congregation. Most of the long-tenure members lack the skills, the time, the desire, the authority, or the energy to initiate a strategy for change. Therefore the likeliest candidate to initiate this strategy is the just-arrived "new minister," who possesses the freedom of the outsider, still has some discretionary time in every month, holds the authority that goes with the office of pastor, has no stake in maintaining the status quo, possesses a strong evangelistic concern, and has gifts and skills in the process of planned change.

Third, it is assumed there is a potential for that new minister to enlist some allies from among those members whose religious and personal needs have not been fully met by the existing life, ministry, and program of the congregation. These members may not feel free to be initiators—sometimes because of kinfolk ties, sometimes because of the lack of time, energy, skills, or authority—but they are available as allies. These allies can help to implement the strategy, and frequently their participation also will legitimatize certain changes.

The final assumption is that, in most small churches, there is a long spectrum in the decision-making process; with approval at one end and disapproval at the other extreme, but a range of "permissions" between those two points.

Disapproval	Permission Withholding	No Direct Response	Permission Granting	Approval

The new minister functions as an initiating leader in the area to the right of "Permission Withholding"

23

and to the left of "Approval." It is not necessary that approval be secured for every innovation, but it is crucial that disapproval and permission-withholding be avoided!

The New-Minister-and-Allies Strategy

While the details of the new-minister-and-allies approach vary from one pastor to another—depending on the local context, the gifts, the talents and personality of that new minister, the openness of the members to change, the availability of allies, and the age of the congregation—the initial components of this strategy can be summarized in four steps.

First, the recently arrived minister MUST earn the confidence, the trust, and perhaps even the passive support of the influential members of the congregation—including some who do not hold official office, but who possess permission-withholding power; such as local patriarch.

This usually means a considerable amount of calling on the members and personal contact in order to establish that trust level.

Second, and to some extent concurrently, the recently arrived minister must identify, visit, and build a personal relationship with the residents of the larger community who do not have an active relationship with any worshiping congregation. Gradually, some of these people will begin to identify this minister as "my pastor." During these visits, the minister can begin to identify some of the unmet religious and personal needs of these people.

Third, the new minister must identify potential allies within the membership. This process should include (a) identifying the unmet religious and personal needs of these potential allies, to which this congregation might be able to develop a programmatic response, and (b) identifying and affirming the distinctive gifts, talents, skills, and strengths of each of these potential allies, including some latent gifts.

These three steps typically will require six to ten months of the new minister's time and energy. If (as is true in thousands of situations) the new minister also serves as the pastor of one or two other congregations, this introductory chapter may take eight to fourteen months. In these multi-church parishes, the new minister also must (a) ascertain which congregation has the greatest potential and openness for numerical growth, (b) determine how much discretionary time can be made available for developing and implementing a church growth strategy in that congregation, (c) identify the components of a "maintenance level" ministry in the other congregation(s) and perhaps, (d) give some initial special attention to the other congregation(s) if that appears necessary and appropriate in those first months.

The fourth step in this strategy typically requires two to four years and is illustrated by this diagram.

By definition, the single cell small-membership congregation can be described with two concentric circles. The smaller circle includes those members (and sometimes a few people who do not have their names on the membership roll) who feel a strong sense of belonging to the "inner core." In referring to this congregation, these people use pronouns such as "we," "ours," and "us." Together they constitute the fellowship circle.

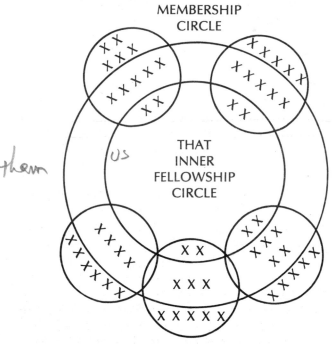

MEMBERSHIP
CIRCLE

THAT
INNER
FELLOWSHIP
CIRCLE

Between that fellowship circle and the boundary of the larger circle that includes all the members are those who are members, but who are not a part of that inner fellowship circle. These members often use pronouns such as "they," "theirs," and "them" when talking about the church. Some of them are regular attenders at Sunday morning worship, one or two may be teaching in the Sunday school, and a couple of others may serve as youth counselors or as committee members, but they do not see themselves as part of that "inner core." This usually

26

becomes apparent when the new minister talks with them. Some of these members have unfulfilled religious and personal needs and can become very effective allies in launching new ministries.

One example of a person in this category is thirty-one-year-old Helen Smith. Helen was born and reared in a community nearly a hundred miles away. Six years ago she married Charlie Smith. Charlie is the son of Ben and Harriet Smith, two of the hardest workers and most influential leaders in the 81-member Valley Church. Fifty years ago Charlie's grandparents on both sides were pillars in this congregation, and his grandfather, Albert Smith, was the most influential leader in the congregation for over thirty years. In brief, Charlie has excellent bloodlines and is firmly ensconced in that inner circle. Shortly after moving here, Helen asked for her church membership to be transferred to this congregation, but most of the older members still refer to her as "Charlie's wife." Helen is an example of a member who teaches Sunday school, helps with a variety of other church work, chairs the Christian education committee, and rarely misses worship, but really does not feel a part of that inner circle. We will return to the Smith family very shortly.

Some time during the second year of the pastorate, the new minister decides to organize a new troup. For illustration purposes, we will agree that it is a new adult Sunday school class. The one adult class in this church is taught by Charlie's father, sixty-three-year-old Ben Smith, but only two of the regulars in the class are under forty-five years of age.

The new minister announces to the governing

board, "Several people have suggested we need a Sunday school class to reach some of the younger adults. Charlie Smith wants to help organize it and I will teach it. Unless someone sees a problem with this, we plan to go ahead and start the second Sunday in September. We're also hoping to reach a few adults who don't go to church anywhere."

Partly because no one can openly oppose the idea and partly because of the influence of Charlie Smith as a legitimizer, no one objects. Permission is not withheld, although the idea may not secure any kind of formal approval.

The new class begins to meet with an average attendance of ten to twelve, including Charlie Smith and one other person from the inner circle, five members from the outer circle, and five non-members the new minister has enlisted to help pioneer this new class. Incidentally, since she is teaching the fifth and sixth grade class, Helen Smith does not join the new class, but hardly anyone notices her absence except the five nonmembers.

A year or two later Charlie Smith takes over the responsibility for teaching this new class. (Ben Smith still cannot see why a new class was necessary. If these people wanted to be in an adult class, they could have joined his class! He is always happy to welcome new members into that class. He does not openly object, however, except occasion-ally to his wife, because his son Charlie repeatedly assures Ben this has turned out to be a great idea!)

About this time, the new minister announces that in response to several requests a new Tuesday evening Bible study group will be organized. No one can object to anyone's studying the Bible, and since it will meet in the minister's home, it will not increase the utility bills, which already are too high. While membership in this new group is open to anyone interested, the minister has invited and secured acceptances from two long-time members of the inner circle, four other individuals who are members, but not in the fellowship circle, and a half dozen nonmembers the "new" minister has met and become friends with during the past couple of years.

During the next few years the new minister takes the initiative in enlisting allies to start several additional new groups. One might be a circle for younger women who are not interested in the existing women's organization, in which the youngest member is forty-seven years old. Or it might be a group for couples expecting their second child, a softball team in the church league, a handbell choir (the money for the handbells came from memorial gifts), a men's service group that helps some of the widowed women maintain their homes, a monthly mutual support group for parents of teenagers, a Young Mothers' Club, a Thursday morning prayer group, a senior citizen's fellowship, a group of parents who staff a one-day-a-week after-school Christian education program (such as Youth Club, Inc.), the team of adults who staff the teaching of the confirmation program, a drama group, a bowling league, a Stepparents' Fellowship, an eight-piece orchestra, a parenting seminar, a sewing circle, a men and boys' chorus, or a Thursday evening study and worship group for people who have to work on Sunday morning.

In each effort, the strategy included (a) avoiding the opportunity for people who would not participate in the new group to veto the idea, (b) establishing a central leadership role for the minister—their friendship with the minister is the basic entry route for nonmembers to help pioneer the new group, (c) enlisting one or more allies from the inner fellowship circle as legitimatizers, (d) including two to four members from the outer circle of members, (e) inviting three to ten nonmembers to help create the new group (most "outsiders" find it easier and more comfortable to help give birth to the new rather than to try to join the old), (f) *continuing* a central leadership role for the minister for at least one or two years, (g) developing new leadership for the older groups after a year or two, to free the minister to help organize a new group, and most important of all, organizing these new groups in response to the unmet needs of both members and nonmembers, not as an attempt simply to expand program.

A reasonable expectation is that half of the new groups and classes will be in existence two years after they were launched. Approximately half will turn out to be short-term ventures or will founder because of a misreading of the need, because of clashes of personalities, because one or two of the leading participants moved away, or for other reasons.

After five or six years, the new minister usually can look back over the results of this four-step strategy and see that (a) the former single-cell congregation has been transformed into a multi-cell church, (b) several new entry points have been created that open the door for new members to unite with the congregation, (c) the average attendance at worship has doubled, more or less, (d) some members who formerly were not in the inner circle have found a sense of belonging, meaning, and personal fulfillment in one of those new groups (Helen Smith was one of the key leaders in organizing that new circle for younger women—when they meet it is not unusual to hear a reference to "Helen's husband, good old Whatshisname"), (e) has emerged some very effective leadership from both former nonmembers who are now members, and long-time members from outside that fellowship circle, (f) that old single inner core no longer has the visibility or power it once had, and most members are not sure who is in the center circle today—and many do not care, and (g) there may be a shortage of space (it is more likely this will be a problem in long-established rural and small-town churches than in urban congregations that once had several times as many members as were active when this new minister arrived on the scene).

What Are the Price Tags?

Every change carries a price tag, and this four-phase strategy for numerical growth in the small-membership church is no exception. There are at least eight or nine ramifications of this strategy that have been encountered repeatedly by ministers who have used this strategy or a variation.

The first, and the most obvious, ramification is that this strategy is completely dependent on a relatively long pastorate of at least five to seven years. The minister who seeks to utilize this strategy and then leaves after a three- or four-year pastorate may rejoice in the substantial numerical growth that occurred, but typically most of that growth evaporates within a year or two following the end of the average length pastorate. All too often, the successor pastor is blamed for the decline.

Second, the strategy is designed for a particular type of personality. The ministers who are most comfortable and effective in implementing this strategy are predominantly person-centered, entrepreneurial, extroverted, high-energy, hardworking, and ambitious individuals with a high level of skill as agents of intentional change. They resemble the model for the new mission-developing pastor described in chapter 4.

Third, it is a more comfortable strategy for the new minister than for the pastor who has been serving the same congregation for several years. As was pointed out earlier, this strategy requires a careful allocation of discretionary time—and the longer the minister has been serving the same congregation, the less discretionary time is left. It is also often easier for a newcomer to initiate new ideas than it is for the minister who has become adjusted to, and perhaps even comfortable with, the status quo. Finally, a minister who has been serving the same congregation for several years may have become a part of the inner circle, and that perspective will usually turn out to be a severe handicap in implementing this strategy.

Fourth, as the years pass, the minister has less and less time for visitation, for the pastoral care of the long-time members, and for identifying and building relationships with potential members.

This may be an especially serious issue for the minister who is also serving one or two other congregations. As time goes by and the members of the other church(es) see the one church experiencing significant growth while their congregation remains on a plateau in size, they become increasingly alienated. Some will feel neglected. Others can prove their congregation is financially subsidizing the evangelistic outreach of the growing church because of the lag in adjusting the sources of the minister's compensation. A few may conclude the minister simply does not like them. Every pastor needs a personal strategy for responding to paranoid personalities, and the effects of this strategy simply support that generalization.

Fifth, this is NOT a strategy for automatic continued growth. One reason is that by the time the congregation has doubled in size, the pastor has run out of discretionary time. The minister is too busy with the new people and the new groups to have any time left over to continue to cultivate new members or to organize new groups. The increase in the size of the congregation also has meant a significant increase in the minister's pastoral-care workload.

Typically this strategy can double the size of the congregation, but at that point, unless other changes are made, the congregation will tend to plateau in size.

Sixth, if the congregation is to avoid the natural tendency to plateau in size after four to six years of growth, this will require a radical change in the pastor's leadership role. This basic strategy assumes that the new minister is both willing and able to accept a "do it" role, to be *the* initiating leader, to be at the center of every new activity, and to be personally responsible for this strategy.

About the time the congregation has doubled in size, one of five patterns usually will emerge: (a) the minister changes from a leadership role of "doing it" to "causing it to happen," and the congregation continues to grow, utilizing a church-growth strategy appropriate for middle-sized churches, (b) the minister leaves and is succeeded by a pastor who introduces a growth strategy appropriate for middle-sized congregations and that church continues to grow, (c) the congregation is able and willing to add a program staff member—perhaps a part-time lay person—who accepts the basic responsibility for organizing and staffing new groups and the congregation continues to grow, (d) the pastor leaves and is followed by a minister who does not introduce a growth strategy appropriate for this size church and the congregation levels off in size and remains on a plateau or (e) the pastor stays, but does not adopt a new leadership role and the congregation levels off in size and continues on a plateau—to the surprise and dismay of some and to the relief of many others. (This series of consequences has been illustrated by hundreds of new missions founded since 1955.)

In brief, this is a useful strategy for the minister in a small congregation, but if it works, it becomes obsolete when that church grows into the middle-sized category of congregations!

A seventh, and perhaps the most significant, price tag on this strategy concerns the subtle difference between "joining" and "belonging" or between receiving new members and assimilating those new members.

Potential Member	The → Minister	Pioneering → New Group	Transferring → Their Loyalty to that Congregation

34

The potential member first develops a close relationship with the minister, and that person's primary allegiance is to the minister. On the basis of this relationship, the potential member responds affirmatively to an invitation to help pioneer a new group or create a new ministry. After a year or two, that person's strongest allegiance is to that group or program that he or she helped create.

If the pastor moves away at this point, the usual result is that the new group folds and the new member drops into an inactive role.

The basic reason for the long pastorate in this strategy is to give the new member and the minister the necessary time for that new member to transfer his or her loyalty from the minister to the group or program, and, subsequently, to the congregation. For some people, this sequence takes only a year or two. For most new members who do not come from an active church relationship, and for some who do, it may take four or five years. The fact that the new member took the vows of membership in year one or two of this sequence does *not* automatically mean that the new member has been assimilated and feels a sense of belonging to the congregation!

As time passes, the minister has to actively encourage members to make this transfer of allegiance. The more personally and professionally secure the minister is, the easier it is to see this need and to facilitate the transfer. (This same pattern can also be seen in many very large congregations in which the new-member enlistment strategy has been delegated to one staff person.)

An eighth, and one of the more common price tags on this strategy, is that, as time passes, the gulf between the oldtimers and the newcomers becomes wider and deeper. In some churches this gulf has become very disruptive.

The best tactic for minimizing this gulf is to include as many as possible of the oldtimers from the inner fellowship circle as allies in helping to pioneer a new group or create a new program. The broader the base of ownership by the members of that inner fellowship circle in this church growth strategy, the less likely this gulf will become a serious problem. It should be recognized, however, that asking the board to approve the organization of a new program does not create ownership. To return to our example, Charlie Smith gained a sense of ownership by helping to organize the new adult Sunday school class, and his mother identified with the strategy when she helped staff the kitchen for the Wednesday after-school Christian education program that included her seven-year-old grandson. Together she and Charlie kept her husband, Ben, from becoming too set in his opposition to what was happening. They have not been completely successful, however, and this is illustrated by the fact that, while Charlie is on a first-name basis with the pastor and Charlie's mother usually says either "Reverend" or "our Pastor," after six years Ben still refers to "the new minister" or to "our new preacher."

This leads us to a discussion of what many long-time members intuitively sense is potentially the greatest flaw in any church growth strategy for any size congregation.

The Alienation of the Pillars

"Well, I'm not sure I can be of much help on what's been going on in the last couple of years," apologized Herman Schwartz. A member of the state staff of the denominational family had stopped in to see the sixty-three-year-old Mr. Schwartz as a part of a study being conducted of fast-growing small-town and rural churches in that state. The two of them were sitting in chairs under a shade tree in the Schwartz yard on this hot afternoon in August.

"Let me explain a little more about what we're trying to do," offered the staff person, in an attempt to prime the pump. "We've been trying to find out why some churches are attracting lots of new members while most congregations have been on a plateau or are declining in size. Over the past five years, the Valley Church has been one of the ten fastest growing churches of this denomination in the whole state. We're trying to discover the secret of your success to see what can be utilized by other congregations. Earlier today I spent nearly two hours with Charlie and Helen Smith, and they were very helpful; and I'll be talking with Ben and Harriet Smith later this afternoon. Your pastor tells me you and Mrs. Schwartz have been lifelong members of the Valley Church. That's why I called and made an appointment to come out and talk with you this afternoon."

"I appreciate your interest and concern," replied Herman, "but I'm really not the one you should be talking to about this. While it's true I've been a member of the Valley Church all my life, and I guess I've held every office, at one time or another, open to a layman, my wife and I haven't been as active the last few years as we used to be. Now that the kids have grown up and are out on their own, my wife, Sarah, and I want to see some of the world before we're too old to travel, and so we've been gone a lot. I think you would be better off talking with some of the other folks. We're glad to see our little old church beginning to grow and, of course, it's great to see all of those young people coming to church, but Sarah and I have been out of it the last few years and we really don't know much about what's going on today."

"I have talked with quite a few and I'll be interviewing others," persisted the visitor. "I want to hear your story and discover your reactions to all that's happened."

"Well, I still think you'd be better off spending your time talking with some of the others, and I expect Charlie and Helen already have told you more than I'll be able to," responded Herman with an obvious degree of reluctance in his voice, "but I'll tell you how I see it.

"First of all, you need to understand I'm not one of those that call this a success story. I suspect that our new preacher is as much a magician as a minister, and when he leaves, you'll see a lot of those new members disappear. Maybe he has produced an illusion, and that illusion is fooling a lot of people. When the magician leaves, the illusion vanishes and we're back where we started."

"I'm afraid I don't follow you," replied the visitor in a puzzled tone of voice. "Everyone I've talked to says that after being on a plateau for decades with thirty-five to forty people at worship on Sunday morning, you're now averaging between seventy-five and ninety on the typical Sunday. That's not an illusion, is it?"

"I don't know the exact figures, but what you're describing may be the illusion," responded Mr. Schwartz. "My hunch is most of those new people really have joined the new preacher; they haven't joined the Valley Church. When this new minister moves on, they'll disappear like the snow in front of a Chinook wind. I've forgotten just exactly when it was, but back around 1951 we had a hotshot young preacher come in here and he almost doubled the church membership in two years. He was a great pulpiteer, he called on everybody within ten miles, and he drew the crowds. Within a year after he left, we were back to the same old twelve or fifteen families. That's what I mean by an illusion. When the magician leaves, the illusion fades away, and you have to face reality again."

"I've heard a couple of references to that earlier period you refer to back in the mid–1950s," acknowledged the visitor, "but my impression is that this is different. Your current minister is now in his seventh year, the newcomers appear to me to have been assimilated, and I expect this is a pretty solid type of growth."

"It's different, all right!" retorted Herman with a new level of feeling in his voice. "Let me tell you how different it is. As I told you earlier, we're gone a lot and we don't get to church as regularly as we used to, so we're not in as close touch as we once were, but we still attend when we can. About five or six weeks ago we were home and we decided to go to church and then go over and visit our son, his wife, and our new grandson who live about thirty miles from here. Well, as it turned out, I had a little trouble getting the car started, so we were a little late getting to church. All the parking spaces around the church were filled by the time we got there, so we had to park out on the highway about thirty yards from the church. That made us even later. By the time we walked in, the place was pretty well filled. My wife and I have always sat over on the right about the third pew from the back. Of course, those pews were all filled and we had to sit in the front pew over on the left. I haven't sat down there since I was a pallbearer for Albert Smith's funeral several years ago. It just didn't feel comfortable sitting down there, but you really can't ask some strangers who are in your pew to move, so we sat down front.

"After the service was finished," continued Herman, "we hurried out because we wanted to get over and see how much our new grandson had grown in two months, so we didn't stop to talk much. As we were walking across the churchyard, a young woman—I doubt if she's much past twenty years old—came up to us, smiled, greeted us, and asked, 'You're new here, aren't you? Would you be interested in joining our church? Or are you just visiting?' What do you think of that?

"Now that really didn't bother me," continued Herman as he stood up and paced back and forth, "bit it did bother my wife. I still don't know who that young woman is, but I expect Sarah and I have been going to Valley Church since before even her parents were born! It sure is different when strangers ask you to join your own church!"

"Yes, I can see how that would be quite a surprise," replied the visitor, "and you've also raised another subject I wanted to explore with you. My understanding is that several people feel the congregation has grown to the point that you either will have to add on or to relocate and construct a new building on a new site. What do you think about that?"

"Yeah, I've heard a little about that," acknow-

41

ledged Herman, "but I think it's mostly talk. First of all, as I told you before, I expect we're dealing with an illusion. When this magician moves on, the illusion will disappear and we'll have plenty of room. Second, it costs a lot of money to build today and where'll you get that kind of money? These young people who've been coming lately don't have it. They're just getting started in life and don't have any money. Who'll pay for a new building? Finally, I expect any proposal to relocate to a new site and build a new church would split this congregation right down the middle. I don't really care, myself, but there are lots of oldtimers who would fight that tooth and nail! I think you can cross that one off your list.

"I really shouldn't have said that," apologized Mr. Schwartz after a moment's silence, "because I don't know whether there are any serious plans for building, or whether that's just talk that's been floating around. The only one who really would know about that would be the preacher and I haven't heard anything from him about it. In fact, I haven't even talked to him for a long time. The first year or so he was here, he came by to call on Sarah and me at least once a month and maybe even more often. I know he's busy with all the new members and all the new programs, but it seems like he could stop by at least once a year and say hello to some of us oldtimers. I don't keep track of those things like some folks do, but he hasn't set foot in our house since a year ago last August. He spent a lot of time on that visit talking about what all was happening, but he never once mentioned any building program."

"From what I've been hearing," persisted the

denominational staff person, "you have a really pressing shortage of space for the church school. You are getting more young families and that means more children. Don't you think those parents will push for some additional Sunday school rooms?"

"That may be true," acknowledged Herman, "but if some of the people who are talking about pulling out actualy do leave, we'll have plenty of room."

"You're telling me some people are leaving the Valley Church?" quizzed the visitor. "How many have actually left?"

"Only the Beckers so far," replied Mr. Schwartz, "but I expect there'll be others. There are at least four or five families that are pretty upset about how things have been going. Some of the oldtimers are especially upset about being ignored by a minister who spends all his time with the new people and doesn't pay any attention to the folks who've been the backbone of this church for thirty or forty years.

"Finally," concluded Mr. Schwartz in an increasingly agitated voice, "some of these new programs are not as successful as they may appear to be on the surface. Let me give you one example. For years I taught the high school Sunday school class. When I got too old for that, Sarah and I started attending the adult class. In those days it was taught by Mr. Albert Smith, Ben's father. He was as fine a Christian gentleman as you'll ever want to meet, but about fifteen years ago his health began to fail, and Ben took over the class. Sarah and I were among the regulars in that class for years. About four or five years ago it began to fall apart. The first thing that happened was the new preacher got Charlie—Ben's son—and one of the other regulars to drop out of the class and help him start that new class. That took two of our best members. Next they asked us to move to meet in back of the sanctuary, and that weakened the class. It was better when we had our own room, but we had to give that up when the new minister split the high school class into junior and senior classes. Harriet, Ben's wife, was asked to teach the junior high class and that weakened our class some more. Ben depended on her a lot to help him. He's not the Bible scholar that old Albert was. Later on, a couple of new people came into the class and the next thing you knew we began to stop studying the Bible and spent most of the time talking about current events or about all the fancy ideas the new preacher has been pushing. Ben was ready to give up the class and let somebody else teach, but by that time the minister had Charlie teaching that other class, and there was nobody around to take Ben's place. It finally got so bad about a year ago that I told Sarah we're going to stop going to Sunday school. I stopped in and explained to Ben why we were dropping out, and I think he understood. He said he didn't blame us, that unless the class got its old room back, he expected it would fold up pretty soon. I guess it's still going, but I doubt if it lasts much longer.

"Now, please don't misunderstand me," added Mr. Schwartz in his final comment to the visitor, "We're glad to see the Valley Church grow and we know that means some of us will be inconvenienced now and then, but I'm not sure the kind of growth we've been experiencing is really healthy. It's been too disruptive. It seems to me a church should be able to take in new members without making so many changes."

"I just had two conversations that have really

shaken me up," declared the pastor at the Valley Church. "The first was with this staff person from the state office who has spent two days here evaluating our growth strategy. He claims there are a lot of people who are pretty upset over my ministry here. They claim I've been neglecting them. The second was with Larry Becker. He just told me that he and his wife have been going to that new Pentecostal church over in Leesville and they're thinking of joining that church. What have I done wrong? Have I moved too fast? Has the time come to think about moving on to another church?"

This response by the minister of a church that has been implementing an effective growth strategy is not at all unusual. It is part of a very common sequence represented as GROWTH = CHANGE = ALIENATION = RECRIMINATIONS. In reflecting on this, there are five points the minister and the supportive lay leadership should keep in mind before becoming too judgmental.

First, significant numerical growth in the congregation that has been declining or on a plateau in size for many years inevitably means change. The faster the growth, the greater and the more disruptive the changes.

Second, unless we are actively involved in creating the changes, most of us naturally tend to react negatively to any change in the status quo. That is normal and predictable behavior—and it always is easier to respond to disruptive behavior patterns when they are recognized as normal and predictable. That is how mothers of two-year-old children survive those twelve long months.

Third, life is full of trade-offs. Many of us have a

choice between eating ice cream or losing weight, but we cannot do both. Growing congregations also are faced with trade-offs. Some of them are the style of congregational life, the priorities on the minister's time, and the interpersonal relationships among the members that were appropriate for the small-membership congregation but often become somewhere between inappropriate and impossible when that congregation doubles in size. Some members who are comfortable and satisfied in the small congregation become unhappy with the changes that accompany growth. Their complaint, "It's different. It's not like it used to be here," is an accurate reflection of reality.

The thirty-six-year-old major league baseball player feels the same way when a rookie takes his job in center field or as a starting pitcher. It is not uncommon to read that the player who was a regular on one baseball team for several years and was replaced by a rookie now is carried as a substitute on the roster of a different team. Some "displaced" members decide to join a different team.

Fourth (and this is very difficult for both the clergy and the laity to accept), whenever the long-established congregation that has been on a plateau in size for many years begins to experience significant growth, the process is similar to organizing a new congregation; with three exceptions.

The similarities include: (a) some of the new members are attracted by the minister and, in effect, join the pastor, (b) others are attracted by the challenge to help pioneer something new, (c) very few of the new members have kinfolk in that congregation, and (d) the new members feel free to introduce new ideas and to create new traditions.

46

The three exceptions are: (a) there already exists a cadre of members who feel a very strong sense of ownership of that religious institution and an obligation to perpetuate the old traditions, (b) there is an institutional memory of the past that may haunt the future, and (c) some of the long-time members decide to ally themselves with the new while others are distrustful of the new and prefer to hang on to the old. That division can be very threatening to some of those long-time members who already feel threatened by the changes that are taking place.

In both cases, however, the minister is in effect building a new congregation, and most of the minister's allies and supporters will be people who joined the congregation since the "new minister" arrived. Most of the opposition comes from members who have seniority over the new minister.

Finally, this scenario creates tremendously attractive opportunity for scapegoating. That may be an enjoyable indoor sport, but rarely is it productive. Sometimes the oldtimers scapegoat the minister. Sometimes they identify the newcomers as the enemy. Occasionally some will identify a long-time friend and former ally as a traitor who has joined the enemy cause. (Of course, the new minister and the new members see these people as converts and allies, not as traitors.) Sometimes the pastor identifies himself or herself as the scapegoat. In other cases the minister may scapegoat some of the oldtimers like Herman Schwartz or the Beckers.

A better approach is to stand back, study the behavior setting, reflect on the patterns of normal institutional behavior, insofar as possible depersonalize the discussions about the impact of the changes, affirm the fact it is a free country and as a

congregation journeys in one directio
members may find that their own religi
personal pilgrimage carries them in a
direction, and keep an eye on the future rat
be distracted by plans to recreate yesterd

A Postscript on This Strategy

While the evidence is far from conclu
experiences of this author suggest that, as
women in the pastorate may be more eff
implementing this strategy than their male
rial colleagues. The most persuasive repres
of that generalization are women in the
who (a) entered seminary after their
birthday, (b) are mothers, (c) are not
married, and (d) are in their first or
pastorate.

The "Why?" behind that generalization
carries us into the realm of speculation, bu
the explanations that have been offered
who also have observed this pattern
following: (a) Women in the pastorate te
overachievers—this observation has
peatedly from seminary professors and d
tional executives. (b) As a group women
listeners than men, and active listening is
most important components for effecting
of planned change within any organizati
disproportionately large number of wom
ministry are first-born children—and
strategy that first-born children are likely
(d) As a group, women in general (and
mothers) tend to be more sensitive than m

48

shaken me up," declared the pastor at the Valley Church. "The first was with this staff person from the state office who has spent two days here evaluating our growth strategy. He claims there are a lot of people who are pretty upset over my ministry here. They claim I've been neglecting them. The second was with Larry Becker. He just told me that he and his wife have been going to that new Pentecostal church over in Leesville and they're thinking of joining that church. What have I done wrong? Have I moved too fast? Has the time come to think about moving on to another church?"

This response by the minister of a church that has been implementing an effective growth strategy is not at all unusual. It is part of a very common sequence represented as GROWTH = CHANGE = ALIENATION = RECRIMINATIONS. In reflecting on this, there are five points the minister and the supportive lay leadership should keep in mind before becoming too judgmental.

First, significant numerical growth in the congregation that has been declining or on a plateau in size for many years inevitably means change. The faster the growth, the greater and the more disruptive the changes.

Second, unless we are actively involved in creating the changes, most of us naturally tend to react negatively to any change in the status quo. That is normal and predictable behavior—and it always is easier to respond to disruptive behavior patterns when they are recognized as normal and predictable. That is how mothers of two-year-old children survive those twelve long months.

Third, life is full of trade-offs. Many of us have a

choice between eating ice cream or losing weight, but we cannot do both. Growing congregations also are faced with trade-offs. Some of them are the style of congregational life, the priorities on the minister's time, and the interpersonal relationships among the members that were appropriate for the small-membership congregation but often become somewhere between inappropriate and impossible when that congregation doubles in size. Some members who are comfortable and satisfied in the small congregation become unhappy with the changes that accompany growth. Their complaint, "It's different. It's not like it used to be here," is an accurate reflection of reality.

The thirty-six-year-old major league baseball player feels the same way when a rookie takes his job in center field or as a starting pitcher. It is not uncommon to read that the player who was a regular on one baseball team for several years and was replaced by a rookie now is carried as a substitute on the roster of a different team. Some "displaced" members decide to join a different team.

Fourth (and this is very difficult for both the clergy and the laity to accept), whenever the long-established congregation that has been on a plateau in size for many years begins to experience significant growth, the process is similar to organizing a new congregation; with three exceptions.

The similarities include: (a) some of the new members are attracted by the minister and, in effect, join the pastor, (b) others are attracted by the challenge to help pioneer something new, (c) very few of the new members have kinfolk in that congregation, and (d) the new members feel free to introduce new ideas and to create new traditions.

shaken me up," declared the pastor at the Valley Church. "The first was with this staff person from the state office who has spent two days here evaluating our growth strategy. He claims there are a lot of people who are pretty upset over my ministry here. They claim I've been neglecting them. The second was with Larry Becker. He just told me that he and his wife have been going to that new Pentecostal church over in Leesville and they're thinking of joining that church. What have I done wrong? Have I moved too fast? Has the time come to think about moving on to another church?"

This response by the minister of a church that has been implementing an effective growth strategy is not at all unusual. It is part of a very common sequence represented as GROWTH = CHANGE = ALIENATION = RECRIMINATIONS. In reflecting on this, there are five points the minister and the supportive lay leadership should keep in mind before becoming too judgmental.

First, significant numerical growth in the congregation that has been declining or on a plateau in size for many years inevitably means change. The faster the growth, the greater and the more disruptive the changes.

Second, unless we are actively involved in creating the changes, most of us naturally tend to react negatively to any change in the status quo. That is normal and predictable behavior—and it always is easier to respond to disruptive behavior patterns when they are recognized as normal and predictable. That is how mothers of two-year-old children survive those twelve long months.

Third, life is full of trade-offs. Many of us have a

choice between eating ice cream or losing weight, but we cannot do both. Growing congregations also are faced with trade-offs. Some of them are the style of congregational life, the priorities on the minister's time, and the interpersonal relationships among the members that were appropriate for the small-membership congregation but often become somewhere between inappropriate and impossible when that congregation doubles in size. Some members who are comfortable and satisfied in the small congregation become unhappy with the changes that accompany growth. Their complaint, "It's different. It's not like it used to be here," is an accurate reflection of reality.

The thirty-six-year-old major league baseball player feels the same way when a rookie takes his job in center field or as a starting pitcher. It is not uncommon to read that the player who was a regular on one baseball team for several years and was replaced by a rookie now is carried as a substitute on the roster of a different team. Some "displaced" members decide to join a different team.

Fourth (and this is very difficult for both the clergy and the laity to accept), whenever the long-established congregation that has been on a plateau in size for many years begins to experience significant growth, the process is similar to organizing a new congregation; with three exceptions.

The similarities include: (a) some of the new members are attracted by the minister and, in effect, join the pastor, (b) others are attracted by the challenge to help pioneer something new, (c) very few of the new members have kinfolk in that congregation, and (d) the new members feel free to introduce new ideas and to create new traditions.

The three exceptions are: (a) there already exists a cadre of members who feel a very strong sense of ownership of that religious institution and an obligation to perpetuate the old traditions, (b) there is an institutional memory of the past that may haunt the future, and (c) some of the long-time members decide to ally themselves with the new while others are distrustful of the new and prefer to hang on to the old. That division can be very threatening to some of those long-time members who already feel threatened by the changes that are taking place.

In both cases, however, the minister is in effect building a new congregation, and most of the minister's allies and supporters will be people who joined the congregation since the "new minister" arrived. Most of the opposition comes from members who have seniority over the new minister.

Finally, this scenario creates tremendously attractive opportunity for scapegoating. That may be an enjoyable indoor sport, but rarely is it productive. Sometimes the oldtimers scapegoat the minister. Sometimes they identify the newcomers as the enemy. Occasionally some will identify a long-time friend and former ally as a traitor who has joined the enemy cause. (Of course, the new minister and the new members see these people as converts and allies, not as traitors.) Sometimes the pastor identifies himself or herself as the scapegoat. In other cases the minister may scapegoat some of the oldtimers like Herman Schwartz or the Beckers.

A better approach is to stand back, study the behavior setting, reflect on the patterns of normal institutional behavior, insofar as possible depersonalize the discussions about the impact of the changes, affirm the fact it is a free country and as a congregation journeys in one direction some members may find that their own religious and personal pilgrimage carries them in a different direction, and keep an eye on the future rather than be distracted by plans to recreate yesterday.

A Postscript on This Strategy

While the evidence is far from conclusive, the experiences of this author suggest that, as a group, women in the pastorate may be more effective in implementing this strategy than their male ministerial colleagues. The most persuasive representatives of that generalization are women in the pastorate who (a) entered seminary after their thirtieth birthday, (b) are mothers, (c) are not currently married, and (d) are in their first or second pastorate.

The "Why?" behind that generalization obviously carries us into the realm of speculation, but among the explanations that have been offered by those who also have observed this pattern are the following: (a) Women in the pastorate tend to be overachievers—this observation has come repeatedly from seminary professors and denominational executives. (b) As a group women are better listeners than men, and active listening is one of the most important components for effecting a strategy of planned change within any organization. (c) A disproportionately large number of women in the ministry are first-born children—and this is a strategy that first-born children are likely to enjoy. (d) As a group, women in general (and especially mothers) tend to be more sensitive than men to the feelings of other people. (e) Mothers *know* it is unreasonable to place the same set of expectations on every person—people are different and that is all right. (f) Sometimes the woman minister who is not married has more time and energy to devote to the congregation than does the married minister with a spouse at home. (g) Many of the men in these congregations have had decades of experience in foiling the plans of the new male minister, but they are immobilized or disarmed by the new female minister. (h) As a group women ministers tend to be more effective in enlisting male support than are men. (i) As a group women tend to be more willing to accept the authority that goes with the office of pastor than are men—and that is a critical factor in this strategy which is based on an initiating leadership role for the minister!

While it would be foolish to place an excessive amount of weight on this observation, it may be that gender, family and marital status, age, and age at graduation from seminary are more useful variables in selecting a minister to implement this church growth strategy than are such traditional criteria as the name and denominational label of the seminary the minister attended, post-seminary continuing education, and academic degrees or recommendations from college and seminary professors.

Before moving on to the discussion of a church growth strategy for middle-sized congregations, we should also note that some of the patterns described here, and especially the alienation of the pillars syndrome and the tendency of churches to plateau in size after a period of growth, also can be found in larger congregations. They simply are more visible in the small-membership church.

2

How Do Middle-Sized Churches Grow?

"This congregation was founded back in 1921 to serve the folks moving out to new houses on what was then the north edge of the city," explained the 69-year-old Wilbur Haas. "When the streetcar lines were extended out this far, some of the members at First Church got together and started a Sunday school out here in the fall of 1920. The following spring, North Church was organized as a new congregation, and the original building was completed in 1922. In the 1950s, we bought four houses to provide room for expansion and for some off-street parking. That eight-room Sunday school wing was added in 1958.

"For nearly fifty years this was a neighborhood church," continued Mr. Haas as he walked around the churchyard, pointing out several recent improvements to the visitor, "but today, except for a few widows who still live near here, we don't draw any of our members from this neighborhood. They all have moved out to newer housing. For the first thirty years after we were married, my wife and I lived within two blocks of this church. In 1972, however, we sold our house and bought a smaller one about nine miles to the northwest. The kids were all grown and we didn't need a five-bedroom house any longer.

"This congregation peaked in size in about 1955, when we had nearly three hundred in Sunday school. Now we're down to about sixty in Sunday school, and they're mostly adults, and we average about 110 to 115 at worship. We're just a small congregation compared to what we were," he continued, "but the folks here love one another and we love this church. During the last several years we resurfaced the parking lot, put a new roof on the Sunday school wing, completely replaced the heating system, and installed these plastic sheets over the stained glass windows to reduce the heat loss and eliminate the problem we had with kids shooting out pieces of glass with their air guns. We also installed new carpet in the sanctuary and remodeled the pastor's office, and the women completely renovated the kitchen.

"Now, that's a brief statement of the history of North Church. Can you tell us how a congregation like ours can reverse the numerical decline and begin to grow?"

"Readstown became the county seat for this county more than one hundred years ago and so this has always been a county seat church," explained the Reverend Sandra Meyer to a visitor. "First Church was the only church of its denomination in Readstown for decades until about twenty years ago when these two denominations merged. That denominational merger meant that now there were two First Churches of the same denomination here in a town of less than 5,000 residents. At first the debate was over which congregation would change its name. That was nearly resolved with the compromise that both would replace the word "First" with a new name when someone suggested it might be expedient for the two congregations to merge. After only a few months of debate it was pretty well agreed the two should merge. A year or two later the other First Church congregation sold their building to a small Pentecostal church congregation and came over here to unite with this congregation. As nearly as I can reconstruct history, that brought a congregation averaging about 90 at worship to merge with a congregation that averaged close to 150 at worship. Today we average about 140, so you can see the merger is not regarded as an overwhelming success story."

"How long have you been here?" asked the visitor.

"I came five years ago," replied Sandra, "and I am the first pastor not identified with either of the predecessor denominations. I was confirmed after the merger and so I tell the people I've always been a member of the new merged church, but I'm afraid that's not been much help. At least half of our members and two-thirds of our leaders still carry firsthand recollections of the premerger days and that still gets in our way. What I would like to do is to wipe the slate clean of any talk about that merger and to focus on reaching some of the people here in Readstown who aren't related to any church. Do you have any ideas on how we might do that?"

"There's no question about the potential for growth here in this community," declared Tom

Olin, an energetic and highly influential lay leader at the thirty-one-year-old Bethany Church. "There was a period of about ten or twelve years when it appeared this community had reached a plateau in terms of size and potential growth, but now two national corporations have announced they are constructing large facilities just to the east of here. One will have 2500 employees and the other close to 1500. When you add the supporting stores and other facilities that accompany that kind of development, I expect our church could double in size within less than a decade if we wanted to grow that much."

"How large is Bethany Church today and how does that compare with past years?" inquired the visitor.

"That's a little hard to say exactly," replied Tom. "This church got off to a fast start, and we had an exceptionally able pastor who was the mission developer, and he stayed with us for twelve years. When he left, we were averaging close to three hundred at worship. My wife and I have been members here for twenty-two years, and the congregation peaked in attendance a few years after we joined. The next minister was an absolute disaster and the attendance dropped to about 150 or so by the time he left. He was followed by a really top-flight pastor and attendance climbed back up to well over two hundred. He was really a hard worker! While he was here, we built the second unit, but I guess we may have overworked him—or maybe he overworked himself. Anyway, his wife felt he was neglecting her and the children. One Sunday he announced his resignation, and about a month later she filed for divorce. That meant we were without a minister for quite a while, and attendance dropped back down again. The fourth minister was a good fellow, but kind of introverted, and we stayed on a plateau of around 150 to 170 at worship."

"At any point in this sequence have you ever had an associate minister or a director of Christian education, or some other program staff help?" inquired Tom's visitor.

"No, that was talked about once or twice, but never seriously," replied Tom Olin. "We always felt that if we could find the right minister, everything would work out. Even if we had decided we needed more help, we probably couldn't have financed it. We were carrying pretty good-sized mortgage payments up until about five years ago, when we finally got out of debt. Three years ago our current pastor arrived, and he is a real go-getter. We've had to return to a schedule of two worship services again, and I guess our combined total attendance must average between 210 and 225. Now, what can we do to keep that curve going up? I'm convinced we have the potential, if we're willing to construct the necessary facilities, to double and maybe even triple in size. What should we do next?"

These three congregations illustrate the first of the three critical questions that must be asked by anyone responsible for developing a church growth strategy for middle-aged congregations. Before moving to those three introductory questions, however, we must define the term "middle-sized congregation." When planning a member-recruitment strategy, it is helpful to classify churches by size, using average attendance at worship to measure size.[1] For these purposes a broad definition of "middle-sized" is being used, and it includes congregations averaging between 85 and 225 at worship. This broad definition includes approximately one-third of all Protestant churches in the United States and Canada. These middle-sized churches account for close to forty percent of all people attending worship on the average Sabbath. Some readers will think of the congregation averaging 140 at worship as a "small church," but in fact it is larger, in terms of worship attendance, than three-quarters of all Protestant churches on the North American continent.

What Business Are You in Today?

Back in 1904, Mary Parker Follet, perhaps the first management consultant in history, suggested to a small company manufacturing window shades that they were really in the light control business, not the window shade business. Thus was born the venetian blind industry. Out of that experience also has come the central question asked by thousands of third-party consultants who have been asked to help an institution or a business reflect on its future. When the railroads realized they were in the transportation business, they began to carry semi-truck trailors on their flatbed cars. When Hollywood began to realize it was in the entertainment business in general, rather than simply a producer of motion pictures, it was able to see television as a customer rather than as a competitor.

The central question that must be asked in thousands of middle-sized churches *before* it will be possible to develop an effective evangelistic outreach strategy is simply, "What business are you in today?"

If we return to the conversation with Mr. Haas at North Church, it becomes apparent that this congregation, after perhaps fifty years of being in the business of functioning as a neighborhood church, now has drifted into two radically different roles. One is to serve a called-out community of believers who come from varying distances to gather on Sunday morning for the corporate worship of God and to reinforce their friendship ties of many years. The second, and perhaps the more rapidly growing business, is real estate—or more precisely the care and maintenance of the church property. It is unlikely that either of these two current businesses will attract many new members.

The two churches in Readstown got into the merger business about twenty years ago, and accordng to Sandra Meyer, the current pastor, that merger is still perceived as the dominant agenda item by a majority of the leaders. The church merger business, both congregational and denominational, has had a spectacularly poor record in attracting new members!

Bethany Church had spent a dozen years in the business of being a new suburban congregation and apparently it was a successful and thriving business. The next fifteen years were spent (a) watching a succession of pastors attempt to keep that under-staffed congregation on a plateau in size, (b) encouraging one pastor to neglect his wife and family in favor of a building program, and (c) paying off the indebtedness. Apparently they never have decided whether they want to be in the business of being a stable, middle-sized congregation served by one minister, or make a permanent switch to the business of being a large and growing congregation that is staffed to reach and serve more people.

These three congregations illustrate the point that the first step in formulating a church growth strategy for many middle-sized congregations is to identify their current role, decide whether or not that is the role the Lord is calling them to fill, and, if they are dissatisfied with that current role, to begin to examine alternative courses of action.

What alternatives are open to these and similar churches as they seek to develop a church growth strategy?

North Church is clearly an "ex-neighborhood congregation." One possibility would be to try to reestablish itself as a neighborhood church serving people living within walking distance of that very well maintained piece of real estate. This is possible, but it may not be easy. Very few ex-neighborhood churces have been able to reestablish themselves as geographical parishes. North Church was organized to serve a relatively homogeneous population moving to that new neighborhood right after World War II. Today the building is located in the middle of a heterogeneous collection of residents. Very few geographical parishes serve a heterogeneous collection of people.

A similar redefinition of role appears to be in order at the Readstown Church. Instead of rehashing the merger, it would be more productive to identify the distinctive resources, assets, and strengths of that merged congregation. When these have been identified and affirmed, they could be the basis for beginning to develop an active evangelistic outreach program. These assets might include: the location of the meeting place, the congregation's visibility in the community, two or three distinctive ministries or programs, a particular skill or talent possessed by the minister, the physical facilities, the talents and gifts of the laity, the common characteristics of several of the new adult members, or the quality of congregational life. The second step in this process would be to identify the unmet needs of people in Readstown, including newcomers, who are not a part of any worshiping congregation. When these two lists of resources and unmet needs are compared, it might open a door for expanding, strengthening, and reinforcing the outreach of the congregation. That could be the new agenda to close the door on the merger discussion and to open a door to a new era of outreach.

After a quarter of a century of watching an understaffed congregation pass the two hundred level in worship attendance, drop back, reverse that decline by climbing back up and over two hundred, drop back again and, for a third time, once again surpass the two hundred attendance level, it may be time for the Bethany Church to call a halt to that game. It appears the new business would call for it to become more serious about the potential for growth. That means staffing for growth. The alternative probably will be to remain on a plateau in which that congregation is served by one pastor and a full-time church secretary and averages 160 to 180 at worship.

Frequently the understaffed congregation experiences two or more of these conditions because of this lack of program staff: (a) new members are not assimilated, and too many drop into inactivity; (b) the total program, and especially the number and variety of face-to-face groups, does not grow as rapidly as necessary to accommodate the increase in membership; (c) leadership development is neglected, and too many responsibilities fall on "the faithful few" year after year; (d) an adequate new-member recruitment strategy is not developed and implemented, (e) the membership curve keeps reflecting a steady increase, but the curve describing worship attendance either goes up and down or plateaus and (f) the "wearing-out-pastors" rate is unduly high. It appears that at least four or five of these conditions can be found at Bethany Church.

All three of these middle-sized congregations would be well advised to take a careful look at the business they have been in during the past several years and begin redefining their role in this new era in their history. In each congregation that will require a change from a dominant member-orientation to a much stronger outreach emphasis.

Frequently the process of redefinition of role is not an easy assignment in the middle-sized congregation. One reason is that the discontent with the status quo often is not sufficient to motivate people to reconsider the role of that congregation. This is especially true in those congregations that have been on a very comfortable plateau in size for many years. One such comfortable plateau is the congregation averaging 75 to 90 at worship. Another is the congregation averaging 140 to 165 at worship.

Who Asks That Question?

Who asks the question, "What business are we really in here today at First Church?" This is a very important issue! It also is the second issue that should be raised in this redefinition of "the business we're in here." It is remarkably easy for congregational leaders to mislead themselves by labeling everything "ministry" or "mission." There is a natural institutional tendency in every organization to turn a means-to-an-end (a building, merger, the budget, staff, an off-street parking lot, remodeling the building, an endowment fund, the parsonage or manse, stained glass windows, a pipe organ, etc.) into an end in itself. This subversion of the basic purpose is a natural and predictable form of institutional blight. It can be seen in government, in business, in schools, and in a huge variety of voluntary organizations. The longer an organization has been in existence, the more vulnerable it is to this malady. The first step in combatting this condition and in affixing a label to it is to ask that question. What business are we in today? What really dominates our thinking and our agenda?

In the churches that call their own minister, as contrasted to those denominations in which ministers are appointed by an outside authority, this is an excellent question to be asked by members of the call committee or the pulpit nominating committee before they begin to review dossiers. The person chairing the committee might ask the other members at their first meeting, "Before we start reviewing a list of names, we need to establish some criteria. Before we can define these criteria, however, we need to identify what business we're really in here as a church, whether that is the business God wants us to be in, and if it isn't, what is God calling this congregation to be and to be doing in the years just ahead of us?"

If this question is not asked at this point in the process, it should be asked by the candidate who comes for an interview. "Before I can talk intelligently or responsibly about the possibility of becoming your next minister, I need to know what business you are in here today. What issues and questions dominate the agenda at your board meetings? What are the priorities used to allocate the money in your budget? What are the criteria that determine how your minister's time and energy is spent? What are the offices and positions held by your most talented and dedicated lay volunteers?"

The candidate, of course, will have to translate the responses to these questions and interpret them, but this interview does provide an excellent opportunity for raising the question.

Perhaps the best opportunity for a productive examination of this question on purpose and role often comes during the "honeymoon period" of a new pastorate. During these first few months on the scene, the new minister can function both as an "outsider" with the benefit of that outside perspective, and also as an insider with access to information that may be available only to insiders.

Many denominations employ full-time regional program persons who are available (sometimes only on a limited basis) to work directly with congregations as third-party consultants on church renewal, evangelism, or the redefinition of purpose and role. These denominational staff members are in an excellent position, as a part of the process they utilize, to raise the question, "What business are you in here today?"

Some congregations, seeking a completely removed perspective, turn to professional parish consultants to help them distinguish between symptoms and problems, identify strengths, suggest alternative courses of action, and raise questions about purpose and role.

One of the most widely available opportunities for raising this question is in the special long-range planning committee that was appointed to look into the future and to bring recommendations to the governing board on specific policies and issues. A useful planning model for this committee to use can be summarized by three questions.

1. What is the principal business we are actually engaged in today as a congregation? What are the priorities and concerns that dominate today's agendas here?

2. What do we understand the Lord is calling this congregation to be here in this community, and to be doing in the years just ahead?

3. How do we get from here to there?

This planning model also can be depicted by a simple diagram.

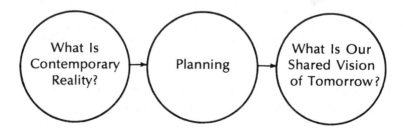

This planning model can be a useful tool for answering those first two questions that often are the first steps in developing a church growth strategy for the middle-sized congregation.

What *Is* the Role of the Members?

The third critical issue that must be faced in developing an effective congregational church growth strategy in middle-sized congregations can be stated in one question. "Will the members accept an *active* role in implementing the strategy?" This is the point at which a strategy for a middle-sized congregation often differs sharply from the most effective evangelistic approach for a small church or a large congregation. In the small church, an effective strategy can be implemented with the active support of only a handful of members and the passive permission of the rest of the people. In the large church, the pastor or the senior minister usually has to take a very active and aggressive role in building a capability to reach, attract, and assimilate new members into each organization, board, class, circle, committee, and group in that large and complex organization.

The key to church growth in the middle-sized church is in the actions and attitudes of the laity. This can be illustrated by reviewing a checklist for the development of a strategy for numerical growth in middle-sized congregations. Before turning to that checklist, however, it may be useful to reflect on four other components of the context for developing and implementing a church growth strategy in middle-sized congregations.

First, unlike in small-membership churches, where changes in the attitudes and actions of the members usually occur *after* the impact of a church growth strategy has been felt, in most middle-sized congregations the changes in the attitudes and actions of the members usually must precede the preparation and implementation of a strategy for numerical growth.

Frequently this means an increase in the level of discontent with the status quo, a renewal of the desire to reach out beyond the membership, and an *active* effort to reflect on God's call to the congregation. Out of that effort can come the redefinition of role, or a new statement of purpose about the "business" the middle-sized congregation sees itself engaged in, so that a means-to-an-end goal no longer is allowed to dominate the agenda. In other churches this means the widespread acceptance and support of a theological belief system that motivates the members to want the congregation to grow and to be eager to do those things that will cause it to grow. In a few churches, the big change will be an end to the bickering, the scapegoating, the griping, and the negativism that have dominated the life and immobilized the outreach of that congregation for years.

What changes must take place in the attitudes and actions of the members in your congregation before it will be possible to initiate a strategy for growth?

Second, sometimes a clue to these attitudes can be gained from looking at three diagnostic indicators that have both symbolic and content value. Do the members wear name tags every Sunday morning? In addition to the obvious value of helping everyone learn and remember the names of others, the presence or absence of name tags also symbolizes the members' expectations. Do we really expect strangers every week? Another symbolic indicator is the presence or absence of exterior and interior directional signs. Do we really expect people to come to this building who have never been here before? Or do we expect only those people who have been here and already know their way around? Finally, do we reserve two or more parking spaces for visitors and label them accordingly? Even more important, symbolically, do our members *never* park in these spaces reserved for visitors? Those three diagnostic questions can be asked to test the members' attitudes toward growth.

Third, the pastor's role, and especially the minister's leadership role and style, are important components of a church growth strategy in the middle-sized congregation. The effective pastor is not nondirective. The effective pastor is a quarterback who is an active participant in every part of the strategy, not a coach on the sidelines. The effective pastor accepts the responsibility of leading, of initiating, of motivating, of planning ahead, but does not carry the ball on every play. The effective pastor in the middle-sized congregation needs to be able to trust the other players on the team. The effective pastor should not try to do it all, but must see to it that everything does get done, and that means trusting other people.

Finally, as was suggested by the three congregations described in the opening pages of this chapter, middle-sized churches vary tremendously from one another. Thus it is impossible to prescribe a comprehensive strategy that will be appropriate for every congregation in this size bracket. A more useful approach is to raise a series of questions that can inform the development of a strategy tailored to the particular congregation.

A Checklist for the Middle-Sized Church

"When I get ready to take my car back to the garage where I bought it, I go through the checklist in the manual that came with that car to be sure I don't miss anything that needs attention. Airline pilots, regardless of their experience, turn to a checklist before taking off and landing," declared Randy Brown, a member of the 385-member Hilltop Church and chairperson of that congregation's evangelism committee. "Why can't somebody provide us with a checklist we could use in developing our evangelism strategy?"

The basic difficulty with this request can be found in the analogy. The checklists Randy referred to are prepared for a specific model of automobile or for a particular type of aircraft. Similarly, a checklist of suggestions on evangelism should be designed to fit the unique characteristics, resources, and opportunities of each congregation. There are, however, a dozen factors that should be considered by the leaders in the middle-sized congregation, but frequently are neglected, in developing a member-recruitment program.

1. Perhaps the most neglected factor is that most middle-sized churches tend to overlook the value of developing a distinctive community identity beyond the denominational label. Growing churches tend to project a strong community image. "That's the church with the great youth program." "That's the congregation with a strong adult educational program." "They have the best music program in town." "Yes, I know about the church. They have an excellent weekday nursery school." "My neighbor is a member there and she tells me the members

care for and look after one another." "That's a charismatic church." "That's a missions-oriented church." "Everybody knows they have the only good singles ministry in this end of the county." "You run into their members in every organization and club in this community." These are representative of the comments one hears from nonmembers when questions are raised about congregations that do project a clearcut identity.

What image do outsiders have of your congregation? How do nonmembers perceive the strengths and unique characteristics of your church?

2. Overlapping this first point is the value of a speciality in ministry. What is the specialty of your congregation? What do you do best in ministry and program? What program do you offer that will have special appeal to people who are not active in the life of any worshiping congregation? Is it a circle for mature ladies in the women's organization? A class for young parents in the Sunday school? A once-a-month sharing group for parents of teenagers? A 5 P.M. or 7 P.M. worship service on Saturday for people who have to work Sunday? A high school youth group built around events and activities that make it easy for newcomers to fit into that fellowship? An adult choir directed by a person who likes and attracts people who enjoy singing? A ministry with the recently divorced? A Tuesday evening study group for people who are seeking an indepth study of the Bible? A Thursday morning prayer group? A softball team that needs some additional players? A group for parents who have suffered the death of a child? A men's fellowship that combines the use of creative skills, an emphasis on mission and outreach, inspirational moments,

and fellowship? A comprehensive program for parents of young children? A ministry with the recently widowed? What is the specialty of your congregation?

3. Who are the folks you are making a special effort to reach? What are their needs?

The response to this question overlaps this question on specialties in ministry. Is your congregation primarily interested in reaching newcomers to the community? Or unchurched people who are having a personal or family crisis in their lives? Or people who are theologically very conservative? Or people who have moved to a new stage in their life cycle? Or self-identified charismatic Christians? Or young parents who are getting ready "to go back to church"? Or families that include a mentally retarded child? Or people who live within walking distance of the building? Or people who have no active church relationship, but are close personal friends or neighbors of members of your congregation? Or people with a nationality or language background similar to that of your members? Or families that include a physically handicapped member? Or couples who recently saw their youngest child leave home? Or persons who are seeking a church with a liberal interpretation of the Bible? Or couples who come from two widely differing church backgrounds and are seeking a church that will bridge those differences?

The more precisely defined the characteristic of the people your congregation is seeking to reach and serve, the easier it will be to plan the details of an effective strategy, to mobilize the necessary resources, and to implement that program.

HOW LARGE IS YOUR CONGREGATION?

"WHAT WE HAVE HERE IS A LARGE CONGREGATION WITH A SMALL LEADERSHIP!"

—FRIAR TUCK.

If the answer is, "No special group, we're open to serving everyone who comes here," it may be very difficult to develop an effective strategy. This response comes most often from leaders in passive congregations that are declining in numbers who find it more enjoyable to focus on weaknesses and to talk about how bad it is. In those congregations, the initial task may be breaking that cycle of passivity before beginning to develop an evangelistic out-reach effort.[2]

4. The next item on this checklist emerges from the fact that the leaders in the vast majority of middle-sized congregations, those with seventy-five to two hundred people at worship, and tend to identify themselves as "small churches." This limited self-esteem often causes them to underrate the importance of various organizations within the congregation. (The big exception to that generalization is the black churches. Most black congregations have a long history of strong and very well organized subgroups and organizations.)

The church growth strategy for the middle-sized congregation should include a review of the life and vitality of at least these six organizations: the Sunday church school, the men's fellowship, the women's organization, the high school youth group, the adult choir, and the ushers club. The stronger those six organizations, the greater the probability the middle-sized congregation will be able to reach, attract, and assimilate new people who are not related to any of the members by blood or marriage.

5. One of the two or three most commonly neglected items on this checklist must be viewed in the context of two sets of statistics.

For the first four decades of this century, with two exceptions, the number of babies born in the United States was approximately 2.7 million per year. One exception was right after the First World War, when the number of births jumped to over three million. The second exception was during the Great Depression, when the total dropped to 2.3 million. World War II brought the unprecedented "baby boom." It peaked in the 1956-61 era. This was followed by the "birth dearth" of the early 1970s that resulted in the slump in elementary school enrollment in the late 1970s and the decline in high school enrollment in the 1980s. Those figures are very significant numbers to people responsible for planning for the future of the school systems.

LIVE BIRTHS	
Year	Number
1911	2.8 million
1919	2.7 million
1921	3.1 million
1927	2.8 million
1933	2.3 million
1941	2.7 million
1946	3.4 million
1956	4.2 million
1961	4.3 million
1973	3.1 million
1980	3.6 million
1981	3.7 million

It is rare, however, and especially in the North, to see babies come to church by themselves. Most of them are brought by their mothers. Therefore, the significant set of figures for the churches is not the number of babies born, but rather the number of women giving birth to their first child.

71

The 1980s brought a new baby boom, but even more impressive and significant is the increase in the number of new mothers. For every eleven women giving birth to their first child back in 1960, one of the peak years of the baby boom, there were fourteen women who gave birth to their first child in 1981.

NEW MOTHERS	
Year	Number
1940	.94 million
1957	1.14 million
1970	1.45 million
1973	1.31 million
1981	1.46 million

There are many implications of this emerging "new-mother boom," but five stand out for the middle-sized church.

First, what is the quality of the nursery? Is it one that will be attractive to the twenty-three-year-old mother bringing her first baby to that church? Many of the young adults in this new generation of young parents grew up in the new homes, attended the new schools, and visited the new shopping malls constructed during the past quarter century. The limited off-street parking facilities and the nursery that "were good enough for us back in 1956" may not meet the expectations of this generation.

Second, unlike the generation of young parents who flocked to the churches in the 1950s and often picked a church on the basis of the Sunday school facilities, a large proportion of this new generation are choosing congregations on the basis of what that church has to offer for the spiritual nurture and the personal growth of young parents. They often assume that there will be a quality program for their children, but that is lower on their agenda.

Third, unlike their parents, who often carried a

strong sense of inherited denominational loyalty, nearly one-half of this generation change denominational affiliation when they choose a church.

Fourth, unlike their parents, who took it for granted that the way to staff the nursery was for the mothers to take turns, many of this generation of young parents expect the church to provide a nursery staffed with the same familiar face week after week.

Finally, a very influential program in many congregations in reaching this generation has been a Mother's Club. Sometimes the group is organized originally by women expecting their first child. In other churches, this is an organization for mothers of preschool children. In many churches it meets weekly, while in others it is a monthly get-together.

What are the assumptions your leaders are making about this wave of new mothers as you plan your church growth strategy?

6. The larger the size of the congregation, the greater the importance of music. This generalization suggests that if it plans to reach a large number of people, the middle-sized congregation should review the quality of the chancel choir, the system for inviting new people to join that choir, and the role of the choir in the worship life of the congregation. Many church shoppers are strongly influenced on their first visit by the quality of the chancel choir.

7. Church shoppers comment most often about one or more of seven aspects of that first Sunday morning visit to what to them is a strange church. One, as mentioned above, is the chancel choir. Another is the sermon. A third is the friendliness, or lack of friendliness, displayed by the members. A

fourth is the availability of parking. A fifth is the nursery. A sixth is the Sunday school. A seventh, and often the most influential, is the follow-up from that congregation.

An essential, but often ignored, component of the church growth strategy for the middle-sized congregation is a cadre of greeters. The greeters should be people who can recognize most or all of the long-time members, are outgoing or extro- verted personalities, like people, and have been trained to remember names. If the physical setting permits, it is better in good weather for the greeters to be outside in the parking area or on the sidewalk. The greeters should (a) wear name tags; (b) focus their attention on strangers and recent newcomers; (c) expect to spend at least a minute with each person they meet; (d) be prepared to write down the name and address of each first-time or second-time visiting church shopper and subse- quently report those names to the church office or the pastor for that very critical follow-up visit, which should be completed within 48 hours; (e) introduce the visitors to members, and perhaps escort the visitor over to and introduce the visitor to an usher; and (f) continue to function as a greeter after the conclusion of the worship service as well as before. Several rapidly growing congregations have classified the position of greeter as the most important office open to a lay volunteer.

8. As was pointed out earlier, too often the leaders of middle-sized churches see themselves as a small congregation, and as a result, unintention- ally engage in counterproductive behavior. One expression of that counterproductive behavior is to assume that "We're a very friendly bunch of folks

here, and therefore we don't need to organize a team of greeters."

Another is to ignore the need for effective standing committees for program. Thousands of middle-sized churches have hardworking and effective standing committees concerned with finances and real estate. These congregations usually also will have a good committee on Christian education. Frequently, however, the committees with responsibilities for worship, evangelism, music, youth ministries, missions, and social action either do not exist or rarely meet. A very significant component of the church growth strategy for the middle-sized church is to develop a system of strong program committees. This is critical for (a) the expansion of the total program that is necessary in the growing church, (b) enabling the governing board to concentrate on broad policy questions rather than be overwhelmed by details, and (c) reducing the probability that finances, real estate, and institutional survival concerns will dominate the agenda. In general, the more details of congregational life are directly administered by the governing board, the more likely it is that the congregation will NOT experience continuing numerical growth.

9. While this next item on the checklist is far more difficult to control (and in several denominations it is directed primarily at the people responsible for ministerial placement rather than at the congregational leadership), it is of central importance. Experience suggests it will be easier to develop and implement a church growth strategy in the middle-sized congregation if the minister meets one or more of these qualifications: (a) has had previous experience as the pastor of a numerically

growing church and/or a congregation that for several years received an average of fifteen or more new members annually for each one hundred confirmed members, (b) has had experience in a larger congregation (many "second-career" ministers were active lay leaders in large churches before entering seminary while in their thirties or forties), and (c) has had formal training in the theory and principles of church growth.

10. While this is the most controversial item on this checklist, any *long-established* middle-sized congregation seriously interested in numerical growth should consider offering people the choice of worship experiences on Sunday morning. The more pluralistic or diverse the membership, the stronger the case for offering people a choice between two *different* worship experiences on Sunday morning. As a general rule, in long-established and pluralistic congregations, consideration should be given to the possibility of two worship services when the average attendance on Sunday morning passes eighty-five. In debating this it should be noted that (a) most of the arguments against changing to a two-service schedule are member-oriented concerns, (b) most of the arguments in favor of two services are outreach concerns, and (c) too often members seem to assume the building committee of several decades earlier is still in charge here, since their decisions cannot be changed.

11. The church growth strategy of the middle-sized congregation should include a review of staff needs. This is especially critical for those congregations averaging more than 125 to 150 at worship on Sunday morning. Four questions should be asked.

First, do we provide adequate secretarial and office help? One of the best means of preventing numerical growth in the middle-sized congregation is to expect the minister to do most of the secretarial work. Second, who has responsibility for the general supervision of the program? If the answer is, "the minister," this may mean that a part-time lay specialist should be added to the staff to carry part of the workload normally carried by the pastor, such as parish visitation or administration or Christian education.

The third question concerns the development, expansion, and care of the network of lay volunteers. Frequently congregations plateau at an average of 140 to 160 at worship, at least in part because the supply of lay volunteers is not adequate to staff a larger church. Sometimes the response is to hire a part-time lay staff person who is responsible for the enlistment, care, training, and development of lay volunteers. The expansion of the network of lay volunteers is an essential component of the growth strategy for most middle-sized churches. In many congregations, such an expansion will require the assistance of at least a part-time paid staff person.

Finally, the question should be asked, "Are we staffed for a plateau or are we staffed to grow?"

Most congregations that average 175 to 225 at worship on Sunday are faced with two alternatives *after* having added that highly competent church secretary to the staff. Some will add the equivalent of a second full-time staff person (perhaps in the form of two half-time persons) to the payroll as a part of their church growth strategy. Others will continue with a pastor and a church secretary and wonder why their attendance fluctuates between 175 and 225 at worship, but they are never able to reach and sustain a higher plateau in size. For the congregations in this size bracket, staffing is usually the critical component of a strategy for *sustained* numerical growth.

12. Finally (and this may be the most obvious item on this list), the strategy should include the preparation and care of a list of prospective members. It is amazing, however, how many congregations that display strong desires for numerical growth do not maintain a list of prospective members!

For every one hundred names on the membership roster, there should be at least fifty names on the list of prospective members, and a committee should be responsible for regular contacts with each person on that list. It also is helpful if one lay volunteer carries the complete responsibility for the maintenance of that list.

As you review this checklist it is important to note that the attitudes and actions of the laity control eleven of the twelve items on this checklist. That is one reason why the strategy for church growth in middle-sized congregations differs so much from a strategy for small churches or for large congregations.

3

How Do Large Churches Grow?

It was the fourth meeting of the Long-Range Planning Committee of the 1800-member First Church. The Committee had been created at the insistence of Paul Corbett, the forty-one-year-old senior minister. Ever since his arrival on the scene three years earlier Paul had become increasingly convinced that First Church had the resources and the opportunities to reach hundreds of residents of this metropolitan community who were not actively involved in the life of any worshiping congregation. Paul also was convinced that the Lord had led him to this pastorate to challenge this congregation to a more aggressive evangelistic outreach.

Out of these convictions came the creation of the Long-Range Planning Committee. Four of the seven members were the personal choices of the senior minister. By virtue of their offices, the president of the governing board, the chairperson of the trustees, and the senior minister also were named to this committee. At their third meeting, the members had agreed to call in a denominational staff person to help them surface the issues, identify their strengths, define alternative courses of actions, and explore the probable pluses and minuses of each alternative.

At this, the fourth meeting of their group, the members were hearing a preliminary oral report from the denominational staff person. After nearly an hour of introductory comments and background discussion, this outsider declared, "From my perspective it appears the central issue can be stated very simply. I am convinced this congregation has the potential to become a 3000- to 3500-member church within a decade, if the members are willing to make the necessary changes and pay the price. You've been on a plateau of between 1500 and 2000 members for more than thirty years. Now the development of this community is about to give you unprecedented opportunities for growth. Do you want to exploit these new opportunities, or would you prefer to remain on a plateau in size?"

This unexpected challenge obviously shocked most of those present. After a brief silence, Erma Wells, mother of three and grandmother of seven, burst out, "I can't imagine what this church would be like if we doubled in size. I've been a member here for nearly forty years and I like it just the way it is. I can't see any reason why we would want to become such a huge church! Why in the world would you suggest we should double in size?"

The highly emotional tone of voice in which Erma spoke impressed the others as much as her words. Before anyone else could speak, however, Erma's facial expression changed, she leaned back in her chair and in a softer tone of voice added, "I'm sorry.

I shouldn't have said that. I know God expects us to try to reach every unchurched person we can. Please forgive what I said. I guess I was just carried away by my emotions."

"That's all right, Erma," interjected Harold Ford. "In fact, I'm glad you spoke so frankly. I feel the same way you do, but I wouldn't have had the nerve to say how I really feel, unless you had said what you did. I've been a member here for over twenty-five years, and I agree that if we doubled in size, this would be a very different church."

"My husband and I have been members here for only three years," added Sharon Frazier, "but I guess I feel the same way as Erma does. We like the warmth, the friendliness, and the intimacy here. If this church doubled in size, I'm afraid we would lose a lot in quality just to be bigger."

"I'll grant there are a lot of unchurched people out there," agreed Laura Wilson. "But why does this church have to try to reach them all? Wouldn't it be better to help start another church? Or, maybe, to encourage some of the other churches that are a lot smaller and need more members to grow?"

"If I had wanted to be a part of a 3000- or 4000-member church, that's what I would have looked for when I came to town nine years ago ago," declared Walter Williams. "According to my notes from our last meeting, we need to receive an average of approximatey two hundred new members every year just to stay on a plateau in size. I expect that if we were to try to double in size in ten years, we would have to take in close to five hundred members every year. Think what that would do to the personality of this congregation, to the sense of fellowship, and to the relationships of the members with one another! We would change from a caring community of Christians to a passing parade of strangers. I want to be a part of a church, not a supermarket."

As he listened to these comments, the Reverend Paul Corbett was as impressed by the hostility in the voices and faces as by what they had actually said. Even more, he was overwhelmed by the fact that his four hand-picked members of the committee were coming out against what Paul believed to be the call of the Lord. He had chosen Erma Wells because he saw her as a loyal supporter who had the confidence of the long-time members and also worked very closely and effectively as a lay volunteer with that generation of young adults who had been born since World War II. Walter Williams was a long-time member, a successful insurance executive, a respected leader, and chairman of the committee that had been influential in bringing Paul Corbett to First Church. Sharon Frazier was a young mother and a very progressive leader in the church school. Laura Wilson was a veterinarian and a strong supporter of mission. Paul Corbett had asked her to serve on this committee because of her special sensitivity to the worldwide mission of the church. Harold Ford was a very conservative individual, and the only person on the committee from whom Paul had anticipated any negative attitudes.

Before the senior minister could decide what he wanted to say in response to this unexpected opposition to the challenge offered by the visiting consultant, John Spencer (who was on this committee because he served as the president of the board) began to speak in a conciliatory voice. While I've

been a member here for less than a dozen years, I
think I know how you folks feel about this church.
None of us want to do anything that would undercut
the quality of our fellowship or inhibit the way the
folks here love one another and care for each other.
We all love First Church. There is another perspective, however, that must become a part of our
deliberations. That is the Great Commission Jesus
gave us in those last few sentences of Matthew's
Gospel. We are instructed to go out and make
disciples of all nations. There are some things in this
world that we do not have a right to vote on, and one
of them is whether our Lord meant what he said
about going out and making disciples. That goes
with the franchise when we declare ourselves to be
a Christian church. If I heard correctly what our
guest has shared with us this evening, it appears to
me that the issue we should be discussing is how we
respond, in faithfulness and obedience, to the
challenge that has been placed before us. Before we
move on to that discussion, however, I believe we
should give our pastor a chance to respond. Paul,
what do you think about all of this?"

What should Paul Corbett say? Should he repri-
mand these lay people for their self-centered
attitudes? Should he defend the virtues and positive
dimensions of being a 3000- or 4000-member
church? Should he silently decide he had made a
bad mistake in judgment in coming to First Church
and begin to think of where he might go next?
Should he ally himself with John Spencer and see if
the two of them could persuade the others to
become advocates of church growth? Should he
postpone stating his own views and ask each of the

others to share any second thoughts they have had? Should he kick himself for picking the wrong people to be on this committee? Should he scold the denominational staff person for dividing and polarizing what appeared to be a unified committee? Should he ask the group to stop and pray for God's guidance on this issue? Should he forget his dreams and suggest that perhaps the first issue to be considered must be how to conserve all the desirable characteristics of First Church? Should he ask the guest to elaborate on his challenge, to offer more facts to support the potential for growth, and to identify some of the changes that would be necessary for First Church to become a three-thousand-member congregation?

In considering these and alternative responses by this senior minister, one must keep three things in mind. First, the option of being a neutral figure is not on the list of alternatives. By how he responds, what he says, and how he states his response to this conversation, Paul Corbett will express an attitude, a value system, and some personal goals.

Second, the members of this Long-Range Planning Committee expect the senior minister to suggest a sense of direction, to lead, and to move this dicussion to the next page. The larger the size of the congregation, the stronger the lay volunteers' expectation that the pastor will be an initiating leader. In the typical large, growing church, the pastor usually is *both* a nurturing personality *and* a very strong and aggressive leader. This is not the place for a nondirective senior minister to ask, "Now, what do you lay people think?"

Third, the next several minutes could be the decisive point in the deliberations of this Long-

Range Planning Committee. The discussion already includes several references to the past and to the personal preferences of the members. Depending on what the senior minister says at this point in the discussion, the committee may (a) begin to identify a basic direction for First Church for the next several years and suggest basic policy guidelines to reinforce that direction; or (b) it may become bogged down in minor details, in debating the past, in expressing personal preferences, and in avoiding major issues that might divide the group.

What *Is* the Role of the Pastor?

This episode and these comments illustrate the central variable in developing an effective church growth strategy for large congregations. *The pastor must want that congregation to grow. The pastor must have a strong future-orientation. The pastor must be able to see opportunities where others see problems and conflicts. The pastor must be willing to accept and fill a strong leadership role[1] and serve as the number-one leader in that congregation.*

It is in these large congregations that the conclusions made in the report to the 1976 General Assembly by the Special Committee on Church Membership Trends of the United Presbyterian Church has special relevance. This report included these two admonitions. "Growing congregations are characterized by stronger pastoral leadership." "The Church . . . must adequately recognize strong pastoral competence as a decisive factor for the vitality and outreach of a congregation."

In other words, while the active leadership of the

85

laity is the most important single factor in the numerical growth of most middle-sized congregations, the leadership of the pastor is the key in large congregations. In many situations, that alone may not be enough to reverse years of numerical decline, but few large churches will show a net increase year after year without the benefit of the initiating leadership of a strong pastor.

In looking at how large congregations grow, one should ask five basic questions. The first, as has been pointed out already, is about the role of the senior minister. The second question grows out of the fact that most large churches already have more members than they can take care of and help to feel a sense of inclusion.

What Is Your Assimilation Process?

A very common characteristic of large congregations is that the membership curve often rises faster than that line on the graph reflecting average attendance at worship or the line showing the increase in adult participation. For example, a congregation may show a fifty percent increase in confirmed membership; but show only a thirty percent increase in worship attendance, a fifteen percent increase in the adult attendance in church school, a ten percent increase in the size of the adult choir, and a two percent increase in the participation in the women's organization.

Many times, lay leaders will diagnose this phenomenon with the comment, "We're having a lot of people coming in the front door, but too many are slipping out the back door unnoticed." Most

Protestant congregations on the North American continent find it easier to receive new members than to assimilate them into the fellowship and to help these new members gain a sense of belonging. Therefore the second most important question to be raised in developing a church growth strategy in large congregations concerns the congregation's ability to assimilate new members.

To illustrate this point, we can return to the discussion at the meeting of the Long-Range Planning Committee at First Church. For many years, this congregation has received an average of nearly 200 new members annually, but has remained on a plateau in size. In a typical year, First Church loses 35 members by death (an above-average figure because First Church includes a large proportion of older members) and 90 who have moved and transferred their membership to another church (again, an above-average figure, but typical of large urban congregations). In addition, every year an estimated 50 to 70 members either move away but insist on keeping their names on the membership roll, or simply drop into inactivity. This dropout figure suggests the process for assimilating people into the fellowship circle is less than adequate. An eight-week survey of the worship attendance revealed that while 57 percent of the adult members are women, 66 percent of the adults attending worship are female. This contrast suggests the assimilation process is especially weak in helping men gain a sense of belonging in this large congregation.

If it is expected that First Church will grow from 1800 to over 3000 members during the next ten years, that growth probably will require receiving an average of an *additional* 200 new members annually, or a total of nearly 400 new members each year, in order to produce a net growth of 1200 over a decade. Close to half of those 4000 new members will be replacements, but some of the other 2000 will die during these next ten years, while others will join and subsequently move away, and at least a few will simply drop out.

This brief statistical review suggests that First Church now has the capability of assimilating perhaps 150 new members annually, but that that capability would have to be at least doubled if the challenge is to be met. This explains why expanding and improving the capability to assimilate more new members often ranks very high on the list of components for a growth strategy in large congregations.

Who Does It?

The minister and four or five allies from among the laity can often constitute an effective team to implement a church growth strategy in small-membership churches. The actions and the attitudes of the laity often determine whether or not a middle-sized congregation will be able to develop and implement a productive church growth strategy. By contrast, in the large church, far more attention must be given to the ability of the various face-to-face groups to attract, receive, and assimilate new members.

Frequently this group perspective runs counter to the personal preferences of many of the laity who prefer to think in terms of individual interpersonal relationships rather than relationships within groups. These individual relationships are very important and should not be undercut unnecessarily, but the stronger those individual interpersonal ties, the more likely the congregation will, unintentionally, be an exclusionary church. Two examples of this type of church are: (a) the small congregation in which at least one-third of the adult members are related, either by blood or by marriage, to six or more member families, or (b) the congregation with a strong nationality and language flavor. For two or three generations, thousands of Danish Lutheran, Dutch Reformed, German Baptist, Norwegian Lutheran, Hungarian Presbyterian, Swedish Baptist congregations, and others excluded folks who did not come from their particular national backgrounds. In these congregations the interpersonal ties are so strong they become exclusionary.

One of the points at which this conflict between the membership-oriented emphasis on individual interpersonal relationships and the gospel's imperative to reach out beyond that fellowship becomes more apparent is in the debate over the number of worship services on Sunday morning. Most of the arguments in favor of holding only one service are based on pleasing the members. Most of the arguments in support of holding two or three services are based on a desire to reach out and include more people.

The beginning point in overcoming this natural and predictable exclusionary tendency is for the senior minister in the large congregation to take the lead in helping the members, and especially the policy makers, to see that the large church rarely is simply one congregation. Usually it is a congregation of congregations—and each of these congregations is composed of a changing mix of groups, circles, choirs, classes, and other organizations.

This distinction can be illustrated by looking first at the ninety-member congregation, in which seventy of the members feel they are a part of the inner "fellowship" circle and perhaps twenty do not feel an equal sense of belonging. The latter identify themselves as being inside that larger membership circle, but they know they are not a part of "the inner circle."

By contrast, the 1800-member church with three worship services on Sunday morning (or two on Sunday morning and one on Thursday or Saturday evening) represents a different set of relationships. Some folks, including several who are not members, identify themselves as a part of the early worship service. Others identify with, and regularly attend, the middle-hour service. A third group, including many nonmembers, attends the eleven o'clock service. Several members switch back and forth between two of the three services, and a few attend at one hour on one Sunday, a different hour the next week, and, on occasion, their schedule requires that they come to the third service. Most of the members, however, being normal creatures of habit, build a relationship with the others who regularly attend at the same hour.

In addition, of course, there are scores of face-to-face groups, including both administrative and program committees, that bring members together across those lines that result when people do not see one another on Sunday morning. Many have the strongest sense of belonging to an adult class, to the Christian education committee, or to a

THE SMALL CHURCH

MEMBERSHIP CIRCLE

THAT
INNER
FELLOWSHIP
CIRCLE

THE LARGE CHURCH

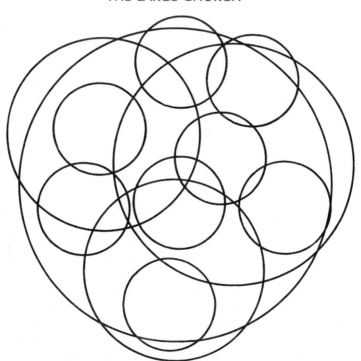

choir, or to a mutual support group, rather than to a particular group of people who worship at the same hour, or even to the congregation as a whole.

This background of overlapping circles and groups forms the context for responding to the question of "Who does it?" in the large congregation. There are three steps in that response—and the senior minister has a critical role in each one.

The first step is to enable the members to overcome their natural inclination to think of their congregation as "one big family." That is the path to follow to reduce the large congregation to a middle-sized church. The pastor must help the members, and especially the most influential leaders, visualize this large church as a congregation of congregations, with scores of smaller face-to-face groups. This is difficult for many people, including most of the clergy as well as the overwhelming majority of the laity.

This effort can be reinforced if the senior minister's basic role is seen not as being a shepherd spending most of the day with one flock and considerable time with individual sheep, but as being a rancher or bishop. The responsibility of the rancher or bishop is to see the total picture, to make sure that everything gets done, rather than attempt to do all the work singlehandedly. Most important of all, the rancher or bishop's responsibility is to delegate to others and to trust the people to whom specific responsibilities have been delegated. This is not as easy as it sounds, if most of the workers and supervisors on the ranch keep coming in and saying, "Boss, I need you. Come take a look at this," or "Chief, can you come and help me on my project?" or "Harry, what should I do about that?"

The effective bishop knows who he or she is and also knows what the bishop does *not* do. In other words, the senior minister's own image of the role, and the role that the pastor projects to others, including the paid staff, can be very influential in determining whether the congregational leaders see their church as one big family or as a large and complex organization. Only if the staff and the lay leadership affirm this complex organizational life of the large church will it be reasonable to expect these face-to-face groups to understand and accept their responsibility in reaching and assimilating prospective members.

The second part of the response to the question of "who does it?" in the large church can be stated very simply. Very few people are able to join an 1800-member congregation. It is too large, too overwhelming, too impersonal, too complex, and too "businesslike" to enable most people to feel immediately at home and accepted. The one major exception to that generalization is the growing number of adults who were reared in a large church, have transferred their membership to another large congregation at least once, and are now looking for a new church home. Many of these people find it relatively easy to join a large church. They have considerable practice in doing so, and most of us are comfortable doing something we have practiced doing previously.

While such exceptional cases are often disproportionately represented among the leaders and the policy makers of the large congregation, their experiences should not be seen as normative. Most new members of large churches follow one of these three paths into membership.

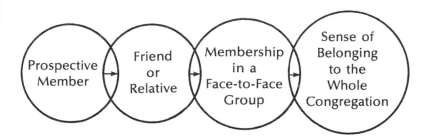

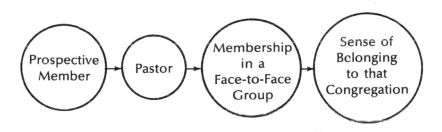

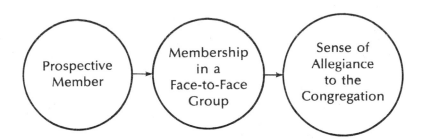

For many people, this sequence begins with the invitation from a friend, a relative, a neighbor, or a colleague at work to come to that church. For others, the sequence begins with the one-to-one relationship with the pastor or some other member of the program staff. For a few, the initial step begins with membership in a face-to-face group, such as a circle in the women's organization, an adult class, a choir, a social group, a committee assignment, a study group, a short-term experience like a church picnic or a trip, a prayer group, or the men's fellowship.

In all three pilgrimages, however, the relationship to others in the face-to-face groups usually constitutes the heart of the congregation's response to the question of "Who does it?" The minister and other members of the program staff can be very influential in helping these groups understand their critical role and in encouraging both prospective members and new members to "find a home" in one of these face-to-face groups. One of the most highly visible examples of this process is that of the teenager who does not have an active church affiliation, but is invited by a close friend to attend the youth fellowship, and subsequently unites with that congregation—and seventeen years later expresses a strong allegiance to that congregation.

It is difficult to overstate the role of these face-to-face groups in reaching, attracting, and assimilating new members. Part of the supportive climate for this role is for everyone to think of the large church as a congregation of congregations— of groups, classes, choirs, circles, fellowships, and organizations. Part of the climate is determined by the stance of the governing board of the congrega-

tion—and this brings us to the third of these three steps in determining "who does it."

What Is the Role of the Governing Board?

The recently elected member of the governing board of a large congregation does not join that group as a completely free person. The organizational structure of the board, its history, the polity of the denomination, the design and furnishings of the room the board meets in, the seating arrangements, the precedents that have been accumulated over the years, the frequency of the meetings, and the role of the senior minister are among the many factors that determine how the board functions and how the new member of the board will behave in that setting. In general terms, the governing board in the large church exhibits five characteristics that frequently make it a barrier to church growth.

First, there is a widespread belief that the board is a group of members who have been set apart to tell other folks what they cannot do. Most large congregations today are suffering a shortage of members who enjoy having the board tell them what they cannot do!

This means it may be wise to refer all questions that might influence growth trends to the evangelism committee. This could include policies on weddings that do not include a member, guidelines on use of the building and parking area, proposals on church advertising, and the possibility of adding another worship service to the Sunday morning schedule.

Second, in a small congregation, a lay volunteer

can be very knowledgeable about every facet of the life of that church by investing six to eight hours a week of time, including Sunday morning. In the large church, one would need to invest sixty to seventy hours a week to be reasonably well-informed about most, but not all aspects of congregational life. Very few lay volunteers can make this type of investment.

The natural and predictable result of that fact is that board members in the small church feel very comfortable acting as initiating leaders. The minister in that small church often is somewhere between being one of several leaders and a follower. By contrast, in the large church, the senior minister usually is the most knowledgeable person in the room at board meetings. Knowledge is power. Therefore, the lay volunteers naturally and predictably tend to look to the senior minister to be the initiating leader. This often means that unless the senior minister exhibits a strong pro-church-growth attitude, the board will do nothing to initiate such a stance for fear of overloading what they perceive to be an overworked pastor.

Third, every one of us normal human beings likes to understand what is going on around us. If it appears to be excessively complicated, we like to simplify it. This natural tendency causes the board members in the large church to think in terms of "cutting it back so it's simpler," rather than encouraging more new groups, additional committees, and a resulting increasing complexity of congregational life. Keeping people out is one way of simplifying things.

Fourth, precedents, polity, parliamentary procedure, and personal inclinations cause many board members to think of each issue in either-or terms, or "approve" or "disapprove." This creates too many "win-lose" discussions.

Finally, in many large congregations the board has eighteen or more members, and thus is too large to function as an initiating group. It tends to react rather than to lead, to converse rather than to change, and to deliberate rather than to initiate.

The implications of these and related characteristics of the board for a church growth strategy for the large church are threefold.

First, it appears the senior minister and/or a small committee will have to exercise a very active and aggressive role in the development of a church growth strategy, or it will not happen. The board can be expected to react to a strategy, but rarely will it be able to develop a strategy.

Second, in order to minimize the possibility of the board's reacting negatively to the changes necessary to implement a church growth strategy (such as an increase in the number of adult classes, the increased use of the building in the evenings, a change from two to three services on Sunday morning, the creation of another adult choir, and the like), it is essential that board members be kept fully informed of what is being proposed and of how the specific action fits into the larger strategy.

Third, and perhaps most crucial, the board must recognize that its power of choice resembles a spectrum, not a simple two-point alternative of approval or disapproval. The spectrum of choice resembles this sequence:

Disapproval - Permission - Active Neutrality - Permission - Approval
　　　　　　Withheld　　　　　　　　　　　　　　　Given

100

This sequence can be illustrated by the proposal that First Church, which now offers two opportunities for the corporate worship of God on Sunday morning, expand its program by adding an alternative service at 6:30 P.M. on Saturday evening, for the convenience of those who work Sunday mornings and for those who will be out of town or for some other reason cannot attend on Sunday morning. What will happen to this proposal? The answer depends to a large degree on how it is presented and discussed.

First of all, if the senior minister supports it, that support must be articulated both early and clearly. If that support is not forthcoming, some members of the board may withhold approval because they do not want to risk overworking what they perceive to be an overburdened pastor.

Second, the members of the board should understand this is not an "approve-disapprove" issue. They may not approve of the fact that an increasing number of members are employed outside the home on Sunday morning. That is NOT the issue here. This is a "permission giving—permission withholding" issue. Will permission be granted, perhaps on a trial basis for four months (during the summer in the North or during the winter in Florida or Arizona) to offer this third alternative for worship? The real approval or disapproval will come from the people, who, by attending or by staying away, will determine whether this was an appropriate suggestion.

It is especially important that individual board members in the large church see the distinction between permission giving and active support. This distinction can be illustrated by these comments.

One member says. "While I probably never will attend one of these Saturday evening services, I believe it is a good idea and I move we grant permission." Another board member might respond, "I always go bowling on Saturday evening and I could never attend. Since I cannot approve of anything I wouldn't participate in, I have to vote for disapproving this idea." Permission giving does not require either approval or participation by the permission giver. (Most parents of seventeen-year-olds have been taught that distinction by their teenagers.)

Third, in some congregations the board will not take any action. They will view the proposal as being within the boundaries of the policy guidelines for corporate worship. If the worship committee has suggested this, and if the pastor does not object, there is no reason for the board either to approve or disapprove. No one on the board should feel obligated to attend that Saturday evening service since the board never "approved" it.

In general, the less pressure on the governing board to approve or disapprove every detail of every program, the less likely the board will be a barrier to church growth. It is unreasonable to expect the governing board of the large congregation to develop and implement a church growth strategy, but it is reasonable to expect the board not to allow itself to become a negative force.

What Is the Role of the Evangelism Committee?

The last, but not the least, important of these central issues in understanding how large churches grow is the role of the evangelism committee. All too frequently, the vast differences among congregations of various sizes are overlooked, and someone prepares an instruction manual that is expected to meet the needs of all congregations, regardless of size or unique circumstances.

Five comments merit consideration in describing the role and responsibilities of the evangelism committee in the large church.

First, that committee probably should not be expected simply to *do* evangelism. Such a responsibility is too vast and too important to be relegated to a committee of several people. A far better concept is to recognize that, by its very nature as a congregation of congregations of committees, circles, classes, choirs, and other groups, the large church is a complex organization. Every dimension of the life of that large church should have built into it an evangelistic thrust. Evangelism cannot be relegated to one corner of that huge structure!

Second, the evangelism committee can be a part of the team that develops the church growth strategy that will embrace every facet of the organizational life of the parish. The evangelism committee might be asked to develop this strategy and to manage the overall process. This could include a door-to-door visitation-evangelism program that would be planned by the committee, or better yet, by a special task force. The task force would design the system, recruit and train the callers, make sure that a follow-up call is made on every prospective member who was identified, and manage the entire effort. Or the committee might focus on direct-mail evangelism. Again a special single-function task force could be created. Their responsibilities would include identifying the recipients of this effort (households in the neighborhood around the church building, the recently widowed, or newcomers to the community), designing a ministry or special program to meet the needs of this slice of the population, deciding on whether it should be a mass mailing or a select mailing by name and address, preparing and printing the message to be mailed, recruiting the people who would be responsible for the special program, and recruiting the callers who would visit every person who responded to that direct-mail effort.

In this model, the evangelism committee has *both* an active initiating role and also a very important managerial responsibility in planning and overseeing a comprehensive program. It is assumed that the five- to seven-member committee will represent only two to five percent of the members actively and directly involved in the evangelistic efforts of that congregation.

A third, and substantially different, role is to ask the evangelism committee to encourage the participants in each program and activity to include a concern for the evangelistic outreach of that church.

How would they do that?

Perhaps the most effective technique would be to ask questions.

The evangelism committee might ask the women of the church, "What new circle or study group are you planning to start later this year in order to reach women who are not actively involved in the life of any worshiping congregation? Exactly what unmet needs have you identified that you will seek to meet through this new group?"

They might ask the Youth Council, "What changes are you planning in your schedule, program, and style of operating in order to attract teenagers who are not active in any church? Do you expect our youth to invite their unchurched friends to become a part of our youth group? Are you planning special events or activities that would make it easier for an outsider to join your group?"

They might ask the Christian education committee, "What new adult class or study group do you plan to start later this year to reach the people you believe should be actively involved in the education ministry of our church?"

The evangelism committee might ask the trustees, "Do you have any objections to efforts to reach and serve people beyond our membership? What changes in the rules on the use of our building will have to be made in order to make it easier and more attractive for us to reach and serve beyond our membership? Are your rules on the use of the building designed to keep people out to preserve the building, or to encourage people to come into our building?"

The committee might suggest to the nominating committee, "We have checked the membership records and we discovered that one-half of our adult members have united with our congregation during the past nine years. Do you plan to nominate at least one-half of the policy makers for the coming year from this newer half of the membership?"

They might suggest to the minister, "Would you please emphasize the good news and minimize the bad news during the announcement period on Sunday morning? After all, that is a part of the first impression some visitors form of this church."

They might ask the finance committee, "Experts on church growth suggest that a congregation that is serious about numerical growth should allocate at least five percent of the total expenditures for newspaper advertising, direct mail to potential members, public relations, radio spots, billboards, and other forms of advertising. What percentage of next year's budget do you plan to allocate to church growth?"

They might suggest to the choir, "We know you've always had a choir party in June to mark the end of the choir year before you take your vacation in July and August. Few strangers are comfortable coming to a party that marks the end of a season. Would you be willing to schedule your first rehearsal for a Saturday afternoon in late August, have a big social hour and thus enable our special task force to invite new people to come and be a part of a new beginning?"

This committee might ask the worship committee, "Instead of cutting back on the summer schedule because so many of our members are on vacation, could we try one summer with a full schedule? After all, two-thirds of the families who change their place of residence do so during the one-third of the year between mid-May and mid-September. Could we offer a better impression to the church shoppers who see us for the first time in July and August?"

They might suggest to the people in charge of organizing the annual bazaar, "A bazaar is a wonderful opportunity to involve people who have expressed some interest in our congregation, but have not joined. What plans do you have for asking some of them to help with the bazaar? You know there are some people out there who feel they have to earn the right to ask to join a long-established old church like this one. Do you believe we should try to include them?"

They might ask the property committee, "Would it be possible for you to install a bulletin board in front of the building that can be read by a motorist in a passing car? The present bulletin board appears to have been designed for the benefit of pedestrians, not motorists."

They also might ask the property committee, "Would it be possible to add a few directional signs for inside (and perhaps outside) the building that would make it easier for first-time visitors to find their way around?"

In some congregaions they may need to suggest to the worship committee, "Our worship attendance is now close to seventy-five percent of the seating capacity of the sanctuary. When do you plan to change the Sunday morning schedule to include two worship services so we will have the potential for continued growth?"

They might ask the minister, "So many church shoppers get their first impression of a church from the senior minister. Could you arrange to schedule your vacation next year so you could be gone no more than two Sundays during July and August when many of the new people are moving to this community?"

They might ask the sewing group, "What are the procedures you plan to use next fall to invite some additional women to join your sewing group?"

They might ask the ushers or greeters, "What plans do you have to provide every member and every visitor with a name tag to enable the oldtimers to greet visitors and new members by name and to help the newcomers become better acquainted with the rest of the members?"

They might ask that handful of members who persistently badmouth the church, the minister, and the program, "Would you please shut up?"

They might ask the music committee, "Rather than continue to function without a choir at that first service, would it be possible to organize another adult choir to sing at that first service?"

They might ask the people in charge of the nursery, "What plans do you have for remodeling the nursery? After all, we're now expecting a new generation of young mothers who grew up in the new buildings constructed after World War II. Many of them are not as willing as some of us older people were to put up with second-class facilities for their babies."

If over the next two or three years the evangelism committee asks enough leading questions of various individuals, organizations, and groups, the members of the evangelism committee may become slightly obnoxious. They also may change the climate of that congregation and cause nearly everyone to become more conscious of the need to make church growth a priority for every committee and every organization. These questions might help everyone realize that evangelism cannot be delegated to any one group or committee.

What expectations do you have of the evangelism committee? To prepare and implement a strategy? To share in the preparation and implementation of an overall strategy? To ask the questions that will encourage every program and administrative committee to be an active participant in that action plan?

To utilize the gifts and talents of persons not on the committee through the creation of ad hoc committees and special single-function task forces?

· The fourth comment about the role and responsibilities of the evangelism committee in the large congregation is about what it should NOT be asked to do. Many congregations, apparently in a quest for efficiency and economy, are tempted to combine evangelism and the care of the membership into one committee. An argument can be made to support that step in many smaller congregations, but it will tend to be counterproductive in large churches.

Confronting people with the fact that Jesus Christ is Lord and Savior, reaching people with no active church relationship, inviting people to unite with this church, responding to the needs of church shoppers, and developing a comprehensive, coherent, and internally consistent church growth strategy are responsibilities that can be assigned to an evangelism committee in the large church.

The assimilation of new members, the supervision of the pilgrimage of new members from their initial relationship with a person to a subsequent sense of belonging to a larger fellowship, the monitoring of the participation of the members, and the relationship of the congregation to people drifting toward inactivity are part of a different subject. It requires a different set of talents, skills, and gifts. These responsibilities should be assigned to a membership committee, not to the evangelism committee! (See item 9 in the next section of this chapter for suggestions for the membership committee.)

Finally, who from the professional program staff

should be assigned to work with the evangelism committee in the large church?

Far and away the best answer, if the gifts and graces of that person are appropriate, is the senior minister. That will demonstrate to everyone that this is a high priority!

An alternative guide would be the experienced and mature associate minister who understands the importance of the task and knows how to help newcomers transfer their allegiance from their first point of contact with the congregation to the church as a whole.

A third possibility is the mature lay staff person, perhaps part-time, who has had special formal training in the theory and principles of church growth.

Last on this list of alternatives would be the summer intern or the seminary intern who will be here for only one year. Just above the intern on this list is the twenty-six-year-old seminary graduate who recently joined the staff as an assistant minister.

Large congregations differ from one another even more than do middle-sized churches, and this is one more reason why it is wise to tailor the strategy to fit that particular congregation. The following checklist may help in formulating a church growth strategy.

A Checklist for the Large Church

"We're in the process of developing what we believe will be an active new-member recruitment strategy for our 1500-members congregation," explained Janet Thorpe, an energetic lay volunteer in that large church. "Do you have some kind of generalized checklist we could use to make sure we're not missing anything?"

That is a fair question. Rather than attempt to provide a detailed plan to fit every large church, it will be more useful to encourage the leaders of each congregation to design a strategy that will fit their own unique local circumstances. There are, however, several factors that arise over and over again, but are sometimes overlooked. Eleven of these stand out by the fact they are overlooked so often by leaders in large congregations.

1. Perhaps the most overlooked factor in church growth is the importance of regular large group events to reinforce a sense of unity, fellowship, caring, and mutual support among the members of the large congregation. These large group events complement the smaller face-to-face groups of seven to thirty-five members that are so critical in reaching, attracting, and assimilating new members.

An excessive concentration in the large church on small face-to-face groups often produces one of two results—and both are bad.

In some congregations the result is what can be described as a loose federation of groups and organizations that include perhaps as many as one-half of the members as active participants—but often less than a fourth of the members. These groups compete with one another for a variety of resources, including meeting rooms, staff time, and priorities in the schedule. The remaining fifty to seventy-five percent of the members are largely anonymous "outsiders" and "ex-members." In such a setting, few members will be even casually acquainted with more than four or five percent of the total membership. Many will feel that their primary allegiance is to that small group, not to the parish as a whole.

In other large churches, and especially the fast-growing congregations, the combination of the emphasis on small groups and the rapid influx of newcomers creates the risk of transforming what once was a caring congregation of friends and acquaintances into a passing parade of strangers. This is an especially important issue if the emphasis is on reaching young families residing in several different school districts. Friendship ties are very important! People feel more comfortable if, when they enter a room, their glance around reveals several familiar faces. This is *especially important with* children, youth, and adults of all ages.

Therefore any new-member-enlistment strategy should include a continuing effort to help newcomers develop friendships with other newcomers as well as with long-time members. Perhaps the most effective single approach to this is shared experiences. (In the old days young adults called this dating.) Whenever people have the opportunity to share in the same *active* experience, it usually tends to reinforce the bonds of friendship. Examples vary from sharing the same foxhole in a war, to working together in the kitchen on a church dinner, to the weekend retreat, to the Alcoholics Anonymous chapter, to eating together, to a canoe trip, to painting the walls of a classroom, to a Lay Witness Mission, to rehearsing next Sunday's anthem (one reason choirs find it easy to assimilate new members), to the picnic in someone's backyard, to the continuing Bible study and prayer group, to the

Saturday afternoon party for the Sunday school class, to the Young Mother's Club, to the Thursday sewing circle, to the church volleyball league, to the car wash by the youth group, to the vacation Bible school, to the children's choir, to the Wednesday after-school program for ages five through fourteen, to the hanging of the greens, to making banners. This concept is of critical importance in helping the children who do not see one another during school hours and who do not live in the same neighborhood develop friendship ties with other children in the church family.

The scheduling of large group events, designed for an attendance of seventy-five to several hundred, and planned to bring people together across these organizational lines, is another means of overcoming this fragmentation and anonymity. One example is the monthly birthday party for people having a birthday in a particular month. This is planned as a social event, everyone with a birthday in that month is a guest. These special guests may be seated at small tables according to the day of their birthday. The committee in charge asks the other participants to provide the food. Another committee plans the program. If it is decided birthday presents are in order, an announcement could be made to encourage gifts for missions. Thus the fifty-year-old might receive a gift of fifty dimes, another person of fifty nickels, a third of fifty quarters, a fourth of fifty pennies and a fifth of fifty silver dollars. All of this money would go as a special mission offering.

Among the key ingredients in planning large group events are several basic components. These include food, humor, music, name tags, and structured events and activities to encourage strangers to get acquainted with one another.

Other large group events might include a combination party and watch-night service on New Year's Eve; a special hanging of the greens service at the beginning of Advent; a quarterly congregational family night with a carry-in dinner; the gala quarterly dinner for all new members received during the past three months, at which time these members are asked to share with the other members present why they joined this particular church; the annual celebration of the anniversary of the founding of the parish; the father-daughter banquet; combining the annual meeting with a year-in-review slide presentation and celebration of what happened during the past twelve months; the festive celebration of the twentieth anniversary of the ordination of the current pastor; or a special seasonal celebration. Each event should be planned to include music, a meal or substantial refreshments, and at least an hour for informal socializing.

Thus the first item on this checklist is an appreciation of the value of frequent large group events in large churches. This can be reinforced by a staff person, or perhaps a lay volunteer, who recognizes that many of the most effective techniques for strengthening small groups often are counterproductive[2] when used with large groups, and who is skilled at planning and carrying out group events.

2. Many of the people who begin their "church shopping" by first visiting a large congregation before continuing their search for a new church home begin there because they are looking for quality. They expect to find quality in the large

church. They may be forgiving of an inadequately prepared sermon or several off-key voices in the choir in the small or middle-sized congregation. In the large church, however, they expect quality. These expectations apply to the music, the preaching, the educational program, the youth fellowship, the quality of internal communication, and the reception accorded visitors.

3. Many large congregations meet in buildings that were constructed in two or more stages. Some of these are confusing to the stranger. What does your building say to a newcomer? Does it clearly communicate the appropriate entrance? How accessible is it, and how comfortable is the building for persons with handicapping condition? If it is not, are directional signs posted at the appropriate places?

4. Name tags are an essential component of the church growth strategy for the large church. They not only are useful in helping members learn the names of newcomers, but name tags also are an effective tool to help the members become better acquainted with one another.

5. If measured in simply quantitative terms, the majority of the large congregations are staffed to remain on a plateau or decline in size. They are not staffed to grow! The accompanying table suggests a beginning point for looking at staff needs for a congregation planning to remain on a plateau in

STAFFING FOR A PLATEAU	
Average Attendance at Worship	Program Staff Positions
200	1
300	2
400	3
500	4
600	5
700	6
800	7

size. The typical congregation averaging four hundred at worship will have two full-time program staff members (perhaps two pastors or possibly a pastor and a director of Christian education) if it is staffed to decline in size, three if it expects to remain on a plateau, and the equivalent of four full-time program staff members if it expects significant numerical growth.[3] This is *in addition* to the music staff, and might include a senior pastor, an associate minister, a full-time program staff member, a half-time person responsible for the assimilation of new members, and a half-time person in leadership development or in children's ministries.

6. A general rule is the larger the size of the congregation, the more important the ministry of music.[4] This includes not only the chancel choir, but also a variety of other vocal and instrumental groups. The congregation averaging four hundred at worship can be expected to include six to ten choirs and musical groups. These face-to-face groups constitute one of the most open entry points for newcomers (especially for tenors!) and can be a major asset in the assimilation of new members.

7. While no one has been able to prove that long pastorates produce numerical growth, it is rare to find a large church that has had significant numerical growth, *and sustained that growth,* without the benefit of a long-term pastorate. The large church usually will benefit from the leadership of a long-term pastor who is an aggressive proponent of church growth.

8. The larger the congregation and/or the younger the people it is seeking to reach and serve, the more important is an adequate quantity of off-street

parking. The off-street parking lot is basically a post–World War II phenomenon. People who grew up in this post–World War II world tend to take off-street parking for granted, while people born during the first third of this century view it as a luxury.

An adequate supply of off-street parking is especially important for (a) evening meetings and daytime events, (b) churches located west of the Mississipi River where most people expect there will be a parking space at the end of the journey, and (c) congregations with a meeting place in a location that is perceived to be dangerous. It is less important for Sunday morning than for evening events and weekday activities.

9. Scores of large churches have found that, from a cost effectiveness perspective, a high quality of advertising program in the newspapers and/or the use of direct mail is more productive than adding staff to go out and knock on doors. The church growth strategy for the large congregation should include an amount equal to at least five percent of the church budget for advertising.

10. A critical component of the church growth strategy for the large congregation is a carefully administered system for monitoring the participation of the members, and especially the members who have joined the congregation during the past two years. One widely used system is to keep track of the attendance at worship every Sunday. A notebook is prepared listing every member by name (it is essential to list individuals by name, not simply family clusters), and a series of vertical columns covers the right-hand side of these pages. Each week, three to five people who were in a position to

see everyone who was present for that service go through these sheets and mark each person who was present. It is not unusual to find this total is equal to 99 percent of the usher count, a far better coverage than is usually achieved by asking people to record their own attendance.

Anyone who has been a regular attender and is absent for three consecutive Sundays receives a personal visit. Anyone who has been an infrequent attender and is present for three consecutive Sundays receives a visit.

A useful backup system is for the membership committee to keep a name-by-name record of each person who joined the congregation during the two previous calendar years. An up-to-date record of the worship attendance is kept for each individual, as well as a record of their participation in a face-to-face group, in a leadership office, and as a volunteer worker. These records will enable the membership committee to carry on a "preventive maintenance" effort to reduce the level of dropouts that is so widespread among the new members of large churches.[5]

11. Finally, the large congregation that is developing a new member recruitment strategy may need to take a careful look at the adequacy of its physical facilities. Frequently such a review is limited to (a) the adequacy of the space for corporate worship, (b) the necessary number of rooms for the Sunday church school, (c) the offices for the paid staff, (d) the kitchen, and (e) the fellowship hall for large group events.

These are important, but the review should also include these questions. What impression is conveyed to the first-time visitor by the exterior of the building? Is there a bulletin board that can be read by the drivers of passing automobiles? Are the signs directing the visitors to the appropriate rooms highly visible in the main entrance area? Does that entrance area include the necessary space and atmosphere to encourage people to speak to one another? (This is especially significant in the northeastern quadrant of the United States and in the provinces of Ontario and Quebec.) What impression do visitors receive when they enter a restroom? Are there at least three attractive meeting rooms for adults—each with carpet on the floor, pictures on the wall, drapes over the windows, and comfortable chairs? Does the building include one such room that will comfortably seat fifteen to thirty people, one that will hold twenty-five to forty people, and one that will accommodate at least fifty to sixty people, but no more than one hundred? Does the nursery convey to the young mother carrying her first-born child that this is an inviting and safe place to leave that precious baby? Can someone in the office see the front door easily enough to be able to monitor each person coming into the building? Is there an excessive amount of glare from the lighting that older people may find distracting or disturbing?

These are among the questions that should be considered in the formulation of a strategy for growth in the large congregation.

4

What Are the Issues
in New Church Development?

What do these have in common? Writing a book. Visiting a foreign country. Murder. Transferring your church membership from one congregation to another. Getting a divorce. Starting a new mission. Firing the minister.

The answer is simple. It is easier the second time.

This riddle points up one of the central issues in planning a strategy for new church development. Should such a strategy be a completely new concept? Or would it be wiser to draw on the experiences and learning of others? Despite what may appear to be the obvious conclusion, every year, hundreds of efforts are made to launch missions by persons with little or no experience in new church development and apparently little interest in drawing on the accumulated wisdom of those who do have considerable experience. This is not unique to new church development. Every day, people all across the continent are busy trying to re-invent the wheel.

One response to that tendency is to ask a series of questions designed to test a proposed strategy for new church development. This approach recognizes and affirms the need to tailor the strategy to fit varying local and denominational circumstances. The approach may also be useful for those who are reviewing or revising an established set of guidelines on new church development. While there is some inevitable overlap, this series of questions can be grouped into categories, with the most important ranked first.

Who Is the Client?

Even a cursory review of recent history turns up several answers to the question, "Who are the folks we are trying to reach with this new mission?"

For the first six decades of the twentieth century, the most common answer was, "Our people who are moving out to the new residential areas." That answer evoked a strategy based on several assumptions, including: (a) the potential members of this new church were moving out too far to be expected to return to the older established church(es) nearer the center of the community; (b) many of them would want to walk to the meeting place, and thus the location should be convenient for pedestrian traffic; (c) the building should face the street, (d) the people to be served would closely resemble those sponsoring the new mission; therefore the style of congregational life could be planned to parallel that of the sponsoring church or churches; (e) the denominational identification would be a major factor in attracting new members; and (f) an appropriate organizing principle would be to send

out a nucleus from the sponsoring congregation to constitute the core of the new congregation.

Dozens of denominational agencies created their own guidelines to serve this set of clients—and this model dominated new church development planning for both Protestant and Catholics up through the early 1960s.

During the past quarter century, a new series of strategies have emerged that raise questions about the potential clientele. During the 1960s, for example, several predominantly white denominations launched aggressive programs to organize black or racially integrated new churches. While this did not receive enthusiastic support from hundreds of black ministers, who saw it as a racist effort to recruit upwardly mobile members from black churches for the white denominational churches, it did mark a new era in several denominations in defining the prospective clientele for new church development.

Subsequently, a large amount of time, energy, money, and other resources was directed to organizing new congregations to serve the new immigration into the United States. As the number of immigrants coming to the United States rose from an annual average of less than three hundred thousand in the early 1960s to three-quarters of a million or more by 1982, thousands of new congregations were organized for Cubans, Koreans, Haitians, Samoans, Vietnamese, Laotians, Mexican-Americans, and dozens of other nationality and language groups.

The nineteenth century had witnessed a similar phenomenon as thousands of new churches were organized by the immigrants from Germany, Ireland, Scotland, Wales, Bohemia, Hungary, Sweden, Norway, Denmark, Finland, Italy, and other European nations. In the nineteenth century, most of the new language churches carried a Lutheran, Methodist, Evangelical, Reformed, or Presbyterian denominational identity. By contrast, the Southern Baptist convention has been the current leader in organizing new churches for racial, language, and nationality groups. Most, if not all, of the net numerical growth of the Southern Baptist Convention since 1970 can be traced back to these efforts. Relatively few of the new congregations created to serve this new immigration are culturally or socially integrated.

The third quarter of this century saw another response to this question about the prospective clientele. How do we reach the people who are "turned off" by the traditional churches? Several methods were based on the assumption that many unchurched people were repelled by big buildings, large crowds, an emphasis on money, or by clergy-dominated congregations. One expression of this definition of the client was the emergence of hundreds of "house churces." While this was predominantly a clergy-led movement, it did produce a variety of unconventional congregations. Most of the house churches, however, had a relatively short life expectancy. The United Church of Christ was one of the denominations that responded energetically and creatively to the house church movement, but by the end of 1981 only one of these house churches was still identified as a UCC-related congregation.

A far larger and more permanent effort to respond to that same question was based on a different set of assumptions. The people leading this effort assumed that the primary obstacles to reaching the unchurched were not big buildings, big budgets, highly visible clergy leaders, or huge crowds. The leaders of this response assumed (a) that denominational loyalties no longer were bringing people to churches, (b) that many members of the generation born after 1930 were not automatically following in the footsteps of their parents, (c) that a positive response was more likely to be evoked from the unchurched if the focus was on the needs of the unchurched rather than on the needs of the churches for more members, and (d) that the most effective channels of communication are now visual rather than verbal. One example of this approach was the organization of the Willow Creek Community Church in suburban Chicago. This independent congregation was initiated by three young men who had been youth workers in a Baptist church. They called on unchurched people and asked, "What turned you off in the traditional church?" They built a program in response to what they heard, and two years later the new congregation was averaging nearly 5000 at worship on Sunday morning. That story can be paralleled by the experiences of at least two hundred independent or non-denominational congregations, each one organized since the end of World War II and each one averaging at least 750 at worship on Sunday morning. (By comparison fewer than 180 United Methodist congregations average more than 750 at the Sunday morning worship service.)

Another definition of new missions is represented by the fact that every year scores of new missions are started with the sponsors hoping they will become financially self-supporting congregations as soon as possible. This hope usually means identifying middle-class Caucasian two-parent families with children living at home as the primary clients.

During the past five decades, thousands of new missions were launched with the denomination and/or a denominational official as the primary initial client. Examples of this pattern are represented by comments such as these.

A. "The churches in our denomination are concentrated in the northeastern quadrant of the United States. We have the choice between numerical decline or of starting new churches in Florida, California, and other states people are moving to."

B. "My predecessor was responsible for starting two new churches during the six years he served in this position. I'm going to look bad unless I start at least two, and preferably three, new churches before I leave office. Do you have any suggestions where we should locate them?"

C. "Our denomination has adopted the goal of doubling in size in a decade. The key component of our strategy is starting new churches. We have a committee at work seeking to find the best location for these new missions."

D. "The office I hold was created to facilitate the starting of new churches. My advisory committee has set a goal of five new missions a year. My job is to identify at least five locations where we could start a new mission and expect it to become financially self-supporting within two to four years."

E. "Our denomination has been experiencing a numerical decline for nearly twenty years now, and therefore we have to start more new congregations, or we'll be out of business by the turn of the century."

In each example the *primary* client appears to be the denomination. As always, the definition of the client influences the strategy and the tactics.

Other clients that have been identified in recent years in the planting of new churches include (a) Native Americans, (b) residents of new towns and planned communities, (c) residents of retirement centers in the West and in the Sunbelt, (d) newcomers to the rapidly expanding communities in the energy belt in the mountain states, (e) persons moving to formerly rural counties to live while they commute to a metropolitan center to work, (f) individuals who would like to be part of a multicultural and/or multiracial congregation, (g) persons moving from the Frostbelt to the Sunbelt (the Reformed Church in America, the United Church of Christ, the American Lutheran Church, and the Lutheran Church in America have led the way in this effort), (h) gays and lesbians, (i) people from a distinctive vocation, such as entertainers, wealthy business leaders, or the military people, (j) single adults, (k) graduate students living off campus from a major university, and (l) residents of large apartment complexes.

Who are the people you are seeking to reach through your new church program? Who are the primary clients? What are their needs? How do you plan to satisfy those needs? What are your basic assumptions about your primary clients?

What Is the Central Organizing Principle?

The second most important issue to raise in formulating a new church development strategy is the choice of an organizing principle.

WHAT ARE THE ISSUES IN NEW CHURCH DEVELOPMENT?

For decades, most new Protestant and Catholic congregations were developed around one of two central organizing principles. One approach was to organize on a geographical base with a ministry designed to serve people with that religious preference. A very large proportion of all new Roman Catholic parishes organized after 1945, as well as most Lutheran, Presbyterian, Methodist, and other new denominational missions after World War II, were organized on the geographical parish principle. Protestant comity agreements that were so popular in the 1950s and 1960s operated on this basic organizing principle.[1] The geographical definition of a denominationally related parish was the central organizing principle.

The second dominant organizing principle in new church development has been followed for more than two centuries in the United States and Canada. This is to organize a new congregation, often on a nongeographical base, to reach and serve a homogeneous group of people who share a common national, racial, language, or ethnic heritage. The result in the nineteenth century was the German Baptist parish, the Welsh Presbyterian church, the Swedish Methodist church, the Polish Catholic parish, the Romanian Baptist congregation, the Finnish Lutheran church, the Italian Methodist church, the Swedish Covenant church, the Hungarian Presbyterian church, the Norwegian Lutheran church, and tens of thousands of other language churches. In many cases an ordained minister was summoned from the "old country" to serve this group of recent immigrants. The original nationality of the people to be served, rather than their place of residence, was the central organizing principle.

In the late twentieth century, the contemporary examples of this same organizing principle are the Chinese Mennonite congregation in Vancouver, the Korean Presbyterian church in Toronto, the Cuban Methodist church in Florida, the Haitian Baptist church in New England, the Spanish United Church of Christ in Chicago, the Samoan Methodist church in California, the Mexican-American Baptist church in Texas, the Laotian Lutheran church in Minnesota, the West Indian Episcopal parish in New York, and thousands of other recently organized nationality churches.

A third widely used organizing principle is to build the new congregation around the personality and talents of the minister. This is more commonly used in independent congregations than in denominational circles, but it is receiving serious reconsideration by several denominational leaders; in part, at least, because of pragmatic considerations.

A fourth organizing principle is to gather people for Bible study with the exception that some of these Bible study groups may develop into full-scale congregations. This organizing principle is still frequently used in the Southern Baptist Convention.

A fifth and overlapping organizing principle flourished in the years from 1850 to 1950, when "outpost" Sunday schools were started as missions by long-established congregations with the exception that in some cases a preaching service would be added and the group eventually would blossom forth as a self-supporting church.

During the 1950s and 1960s a new organizing principle was added to the list. This was the advance purchase of the land for a new congregation's meeting place and the erection of a prominent sign advertising that eventually a congregation of that denomination would be meeting at this location. Apparently it was hoped the sign and the promise would draw potential new members.

An overlapping concept was to construct the new building on that site and send a minister (often on a part-time schedule) to welcome and preach to the folks attracted by the new building. While it usually had only limited success, this organizing principle was more effective in the efforts during the 1950s to attract the young parents from the survival-oriented generation born in the 1920s than in reaching a different generation of people born after 1940.

A parallel approach was the satellite concept that flourished in the 1960s and early 1970s. The long-established downtown congregation, concluding that its location in the central business district would keep it from attracting young families living in new houses several miles away, would purchase a parcel of land out in a new residential area. On this site, a general purpose building would be constructed, and an outreach to nearby residents would be launched. The typical pattern was for an early Sunday morning worship service to be scheduled at the satellite with a later service at the older building downtown. Sunday school classes would be held at both locations. New members would be carried on the roll of the sponsoring church. The whole operation would usually continue as one congregation with one set of officers, one staff, one budget, and one program, but with two locations. Typically, the expectations that "the folks out at the satellite will come downtown" for other events, programs, and meetings were not realized.

The satellite approach was a rational, logical, and economical approach to evangelism, but it overlooked the attachment of people to place, perhaps the most neglected factor in church planning.[2] Typically, the number of people who identified with the satellite did not increase as rapidly as had been anticipated. Usually about five years after such a plan was launched, the satellite congregation would reorganize as a separate congregation. In a few cases the "mother church" sold its old meeting place and moved in with the "daughter church."

In the early 1970s, another organizing principle became more visible as thousands of new congregations were started to serve a theologically homogeneous group of people. Many of these were developed to serve self-identified charismatic Christians. Others organized because the founders were convinced that no other churches in their community were faithful and obedient in preaching and teaching the pure word of God. Hundreds were started as nondenominational churches, while more than a few were organized around an antidenominational stance.

In some of these, the oldest organizing principle known to humankind—to identify and organize against the enemy—was used to build a group of individuals into a closely knit and cohesive group.

Finally (although it overlaps the previous question on the identification of the primary client), one other organizing principle must be mentioned here. During the late 1960s, several national denominational missions agencies developed a systematic strategy to reach people who were not actively involved in the life of any worshiping congregation. In many cases, the central organizing principle was to build the new mission around the magnetic personality of the mission developer pastor. In others, however, the central organizing principle was based on (a) the fact that most people prefer to help give birth to something new rather than attempt to join and perpetuate an old organization, and (b) the fact that people with no active church relationship have needs that can be identified and a new congregation has the freedom to shape its ministry in response to those needs, rather than in response to the pressures of yesterday's traditions. The pioneers determine the priorities and the agenda for the new mission.

What is the central organizing principle you expect to use in planting a new church? To bring together people from a common denominational heritage? To serve a geographical community regardless of the denominational background of the people? To develop a new language or nationality church? To rally people around the organizing pastor? To organize against the enemy? To gather people for Bible study? To start an outpost from an existing church? To focus your efforts on people with no active church relationship? To invite people to help pioneer a new venture?

Start Small and Grow, or Start Big?

A third issue in developing a strategy for planting new churches reflects two radically different approaches. Traditionally, the approach has been to organize a new mission with anywhere from a dozen families up to as many as sixty or seventy individuals. This small nucleus would be expected to grow into a larger congregation. This meant that both the congregation and the mission developer pastor were expected to progress through several developmental stages. In some cases, the dream was fulfilled. In a majority of these efforts, however, the new mission hit a plateau and remained on that plateau in size. The minister and/or the members were unable to make the necessary changes in leadership role and in congregational lifestyle to continue to grow in numbers. Some leveled off with 45 people, more or less, at worship. Others found a comfortable plateau with appoximately 85 at worship, and a few found that uncomfortable plateau with 110 to 125 at worship, but did not fulfill the original expectations.

An alternative approach has been to find a person-centered, extroverted, dynamic, aggressive, entrepreneurial minister and send that magnetic personality out with three instructions. First, spend six to ten months meeting as many people as you can and building friendship ties with them. Concentrate your time and energy on people who do not have any active church relationship. Make at least six calls on each prospective member before scheduling that first worship service. Second, do not schedule your first worship service until you are confident you will have at least two hundred people in attendance. Third, expect that to be the smallest crowd you will ever have for Sunday morning worship.

A comparison of these two approaches suggests that it is easier for both the members and the minister to begin as a large church than it is to start small and move through several stages of size.

There, of course, are some exceptions to this generalization. In general, congregations drawn from upwardly mobile people in the upper half of the socio-economic slice of the population tend to be larger. Hispanic congregations tend to be small. Working-class people tend to prefer smaller congregations. Mature adults tend to prefer smaller congregations.

Are you planning to start small and grow? Or to start small and stay small? Or to start large? Which approach is compatible with the people you are seeking to reach? Which is compatible with your central organizing principle? Which is compatible with your overall strategy?

Who Will Be the Pastor?

Overlapping that last issue is the subject that many denominational leaders place at the top of the list. Who will be the mission developer pastor? Much has been written on this subject but there still remain big differences of opinion.[3] In addition to the normal expectations in regard to Christian commitment, training, family support, personality, and similar characteristics, five observations merit special consideration here.

First, many of the personal and professional characteristics that are appropriate and helpful for the pastor of a long-established congregation are not necessarily the most important talents of a new church developer. Some ministers who do not "fit" into the life of the long-established and stable congregation make excellent new church pastors.

Likewise, some effective mission developers encounter severe difficulties when they move to become the fourth or fourteenth pastor of a long-established church.

Second, there is increasing agreement that the ministers who are most effective in quickly building a comparatively large new congregation that soon becomes financially self-supporting display a high level of entrepreneurial skill. They are enterprising individuals. Their critics refer to them as empire builders. They often resemble such well known, controversial, and entrepreneurial figures as Hyman Rickover, J. Edgar Hoover, and Robert Moses, each one of whom was remarkably skilled at altering the traditional rules on the allocation of scarce resources.[4] They possess an incredible desire to succeed. They are willing to make major personal sacrifices of time and energy in order to achieve their goals. They are confident risk-takers. They possess a strong independent streak and usually do not fit comfortably into a bureaucratic structure. Many have had experience in door-to-door sales before going into the ordained ministry. They are able to rehearse mentally future actions and events and practice what is sometimes referred to as mental rehearsal—a concept utilized by most baseball managers and football coaches. They want to be independent and self-sufficient, but they also know how to delegate and take vacations, and they can manage stress. They usually are remarkably persuasive. They are optimistic about the future and rarely look back. They are self-starters and are guided by compelling internal goals. They are very realistic about the world in which they find themselves. They tend to solve problems, rather than search for scapegoats. Some identify themselves as "inventors." They like people. They know how to manage their own time. They rarely make good associate ministers or fit into a collegial team structure, but they make very effective new church developers! In terms of personality characteristics, they are unlike most of the students enrolling in denominational seminaries in the 1960s and early 1970s.

Third, the most effective new mission developers are able and willing to take the initiative in meeting strangers. They can see the potential in people. They are the ones who say "Hello!" first. They know how to build relationships with strangers by concentrating on the concerns and needs of the other person, by actively listening to the other person. They act on the assumption that anyone who joined that new mission did so intentionally and expects to be actively involved in that pioneering venture.

Fourth, the new mission pastor should understand the concept of the "transformational" leadership role. This role (according to its chief advocate) calls for the leader to look beyond current needs and demands and to be able to see a new era that will be different from the contemporary scene.[5]

An understanding of the transformational leadership role is especially significant if (a) the strategy calls for beginning with a small number of people and transforming that group into a large congregation, and/or (b) the original mission developer will be expected to stay for a long pastorate. There are four major transformations that often can be identified in the church that was once a new mission. These are (1) the transformation in the role of the mission developer pastor from a "shepherd"

137

to a "rancher," from being *the* leader to functioning as the professional leader who can delegate responsibilities to others; (2) the transformation from the "one big family" style of congregational life in which the governing board (session, council, vestry, and the like) carries most of the administrative and program responsibilities into a more complex organizational structure with a network of committees and a supervisory role for the central governing body; (3) the transformation in the self-image of the members from "We're just a small new mission" into "We're a large, complex, and maturing congregation"; and (4) the transformation from the concentration during those early years on specific, attainable, measurable, visible, unifying, and satisfying "survival" goals to a subsequent emphasis on more subjective, and sometimes divisive, ministry goals. The minister who continues for a decade or longer as the pastor of a new mission is almost certain to be faced with the challenge of at least three of these changes. The transformational leadership role is required at each of those points in the evolution of what once was a new mission.

Finally, the people who are most effective in planting new congregations have their career ahead of them, are full-time, do not serve any other congregation, accepted the assignment because of the challenge (not because they simply wanted to escape from where they were), and were willing to be initiating leaders. In other words, the retired minister, the introverted personality, the minister serving another congregation on a part-time basis, the self-styled enabler, or the minister who is under pressure to relocate are not the best candidates for this responsibility.

138

Do We Need a Full-Time Pastor?

The last three decades have witnessed hundreds of efforts to organize new congregations with part-time pastoral leadership. In many cases, this was an effort to save money. The pastor of a small and long-established stable congregation was asked to be the minister for a new mission. The associate minister of the downtown church was assigned, on a part-time basis, to organize a new church. A part-time student pastor, or a retired minister, was secured at considerable savings. In other organizing efforts, the focus was on the ministry of the laity, and the organizers assumed that a part-time ordained minister would, of necessity, enhance the role of the laity.

These experiences suggest that obtaining a full-time pastor is the appropriate route to follow if (a) the objective is to develop a congregation averaging more than 150 at worship, (b) the central organizing principle is to build the congregation around the personality of the pastor, (c) denominational resources for long-term subsidies are limited, (d) the focus is on reaching people from the upper half of the socio-economic division of the population, and/or (e) the primary clientele are people who work for others and/or people born after 1940.

Having a part-time minister may be more appropriate if (a) the church is expected to be a small-membership church, (b) it is desirable to maintain a long-term dependence on denominational headquarters, (c) the denominational polity and tradition stress the role of the laity (Mennonite, Quakers, Baptist, and Mormons) and (d) the central focus is on reaching self-employed people and/or unskilled and semi-skilled members of the labor force.

In deciding whether the denominational leaders (or sponsoring church) will select the minister, or whether the prospective members of the new mission will have that authority, a subtle distinction should be kept in mind. To members of the new mission, there is a big difference between choosing the new minister and approving someone else's choice. That distinction is especially important if most of the new members were born after 1940 and are less responsive to authority figures.

How Much Subsidy?

Perhaps the most complicated issue on this agenda is the question of financial subsidies to new congregations.

There are a half-dozen generalizations that provide a context for looking a this issue.

First, in the American culture, the established tradition has been to subsidize homeowners, wealthy people, and others from the upper half of the economic distribution of the population. Milton and Rose Friedman, for example, have pointed out that children from well-to-do families benefit disproportionately from the subsidies for higher education in the United States, while poor families provide a larger subsidy for higher education than their children receive.[6] Well-to-do people expect to be subsidized by the larger society. This generalization helps explain one of the basic rules in new church development. The higher the income level of the people to be served, the larger the

denominational subsidy they will expect. Among the new churches with the largest denominational subsidies are those that were started in Columbia, Maryland, a community with one of the highest levels of family income in the nation. By contrast, the majority of all new black or new Hispanic congregations started in Texas, Illinois, California, New York, or Michigan in 1982 did not receive a nickel in denominational subsidies.

Second, while it once was assumed that the values of the helped and the helper coincided, it has become increasingly apparent in recent years that subsidies often encourage the emergence of an adversary relationship. A simple example is the case of the leaders of the "new" mission that has been subsidized by the denomination for the past nine years who spend considerable time and energy every year preparing their brief for the mission board to prove the need for a continuation of that financial subsidy. These hearings often take the form of an adversary procedure. There is an old bit of wisdom that declares, "Dependency fosters hostility." That generalization often applies to new church development.

Third, in general, numerical growth and financial subsidies are incompatible. Whether the subsidy to the operating budget or the minister's salary comes from an endowment fund or from denominational sources, it is rare to find a congregation that has been receiving financial subsidies for more than three or four years and is also experiencing significant numerical growth.

Fourth, financial subsidies coming directly from other congregations appear to have less of a negative impact on a new mission than those that

"DEPENDENCY CAN CREATE HOSTILITY (GULP)!"

—FRIAR TUCK.

come via denominational channels. Examples of the operational implementation of this concept include: (a) the older congregation that purchases the land for a new mission, (b) the church builders club that provides the money for purchase of the land for a new mission, (c) the one-time grant by one or more churches to match the receipts from the new mission's building fund drive among its own members for the construction of a permanent meeting place, or (d) the decision by a large congregation to provide most or all of the compensation for the mission developer pastor for one or two years. It appears that denominational agencies are more reluctant to terminate financial subsidies than are sister congregations.

Fifth, in several of the predominantly Anglo-Protestant denominations, the issue of financial subsidies for minority churches often becomes a power struggle over who will have the control over the allocation—and potential withdrawal—of that financial subsidy, rather than over the criteria to be used in deciding on the amount and the use of those funds.

Finally (in general), the longer the anticipated period of financial subsidy, the slower the growth rate and/or the more likely the new mission will plateau in size with less than one hundred at worship on Sunday morning. Some denominations have a history of promising subsidies for seven to twelve years if needed. Other denominations categorically promise a maximum of three years of financial assistance to the new mission. The record of the second approach is far more impressive than the record of long-term subsidies.

There appears to be increasing agreement among

denominational leaders that a three-year financial subsidy, with a decreasing amount each year, is the most that can be granted without adversely affecting the health and vitality of the new congregation.

What are your assumptions about financial subsidies for new congregations?[7] Do your policies agree with your assumptions?

How Large Should the Nucleus Be?

One traditional approach to new church development has been to send out a group of members from the sponsoring church to constitute the nucleus of the new mission. This means the new congregation begins with a large group—typically between fifty and two hundred people—who are committed Christians and knowledgeable church leaders enthusiastic about helping to pioneer a new church. Together they often are able to contribute a substantial sum of money in order to minimize outside subsidies for operating expenses.

After one looks at several dozen such ventures, three issues emerge that suggest reconsideration of this approach.

First, this system tends to produce a "clone"—a new congregation that resembles the sponsoring church, except that the median age usually is younger and there may be more families with young children. As a result of the workings of the homogeneous unit principle,[8] the new church tends to reach people who resemble the people in the nucleus. Frequently it has not been an effective means of reaching unchurched people or of

145

reaching people who were not reached by the sponsoring church.

Second, in some of these efforts, the group going out from the sponsoring church (a) were close personal friends with one another, (b) were numerous enough to constitute a new congregation and did not need the help of any "outsiders," (c) had agreed among themselves on a precisely defined model of the new congregation and did not need the suggestions or ideas of any outsiders, (d) were able to mobilize the necessary financial resources from among their own numbers and their friends back at the sponsoring church, and (e) successfully discouraged any outsiders from joining their fellowship.

Third, the people volunteering to constitute the nucleus for the new church tended NOT to be a representative cross-section of the membership of the sponsoring church. Those going out tended to be younger, more venturesome, more likely to have children at home, and to have a strong future orientation. Those left behind tended to be older, without children at home, less venturesome, and to have a stronger orientation to the past.

The departure of the nucleus often produced one of these results in the sponsoring church: (a) it lost its family orientation and defined a new role for itself as a congregation with a ministry with mature adults; (b) it lost its family orientation and, failing to define a new role for itself,[9] began a long period of numerical decline; (c) the departure "of all those young families" gave the leaders at the sponsoring church a plausible excuse for explaining why nothing was happening and why their congregation was declining; (d) the new mission grew so rapidly that the leaders at the sponsoring church saw the wisdom of that action and voted to relocate to a site a short distance from the new mission and compete with it for those attractive young families; or (e) the leaders at the downtown church watched the new church grow and flourish, and on the basis of the old slogan, "If you can't beat 'em, join 'em," voted to merge with the new congregation at the new mission's meeting place.

This scenario reminds one of Woody Hayes' response when asked why the Ohio State University football team did not rely more on the forward pass. Hayes replied that when the quarterback fades back to pass, one of four things will happen, and three of them are bad.

If the sponsor-church concept is to be followed, the ideal number to send out from the mother church is somewhere between zero and two. The exact number will depend on whether the pastor sent to start the new church is a member of the sponsoring congregation, and whether that pastor's spouse is a member of the sponsoring congregation.

In general, the smaller the nucleus, the greater the probability that the new mission will reach people who are not actively involved in any congregation. The larger the nucleus, the greater the probability the new members of the new mission will resemble the people in that nucleus.

The strongest advocates of sending out a nucleus are those who want to reproduce a series of congregations that closely resemble the mother church. The skeptics come largely from among those who are comfortable with a more pluralistic approach to evangelism. What is your stance? Is "cloning" compatible with your goals and your values?

Who Will Enlist the New Members?

One of the most frequently used arguments in favor of beginning with a nucleus of persons from another congregation is that it avoids the issue of enlisting a cadre of strangers as new members. If, however, the focus is on reaching people who are not active in any church, the question surfaces, Who will enlist the new members?

The usual candidate for this job is the mission-developer pastor who will call door-to-door. Perhaps the lowest-cost solution, in the long run, is to give that responsibility to the mission-developer pastor for six to eight months (or until 200 to 300 potential members have been identified from the unchurched population), to begin holding worship services, to organize the rest of the program, and to bring in a trained parish visitor who will share with the pastor the responsibility for enlisting the next three to five hundred members.

A third alternative is for the mission-developer pastor to enlist the first one hundred to two hundred new members, and from that group, identify and train eight to twelve lay volunteers who have the gifts appropriate for visitation evangelism.

A fourth alternative is to organize, from members of sister churches, a cadre of people who will be trained to make several thousand telephone calls to identify potential members to be visited by the mission developer. This tactic requires (among other preparations) a training program for the callers and a script the callers must follow in making their calls.

A few denominations ask members of sister churches to do the door-to-door calling, but that creates credibility problems when the person(s) being visited discovers the caller has no intention of joining the new mission. Salespeople do better if they use the product they are selling.

Some new missions are being organized around a specific program, such as a Christian Day School, a ministry with single adults, or a ministry with families that include a handicapped member.

Perhaps the worst method of starting a new mission is for one lay person to bring together singlehandedly ten to twenty people who will be the first new members. All too often, this has meant that the new pastor, who arrives several weeks later, is perceived as a trespasser, rather than as one of the original pioneers. The more effective the new minister is at bringing new people into the group, the greater the risk of alienating the members of that original core. The new minister also may be perceived as crowding the lay person who started the process out of the spotlight. Finally, this method runs the risk of attracting some people to that original cadre who are personally incompatible with the new minister.

How will the new missions you are planning enlist new members?

Do We Need Our Own Land and Building?

For at least three decades, church leaders have been frustrated by the rising costs of land for new missions and for the construction of buildings. One alternative, followed by thousands of new congregations serving people from the lower half of the income structure, has been to use temporary facilities until they are able to purchase a church building being abandoned by a congregation serving a wealthier segment of the population. This alternative has been chosen by a very large number of fundamentalist, holiness, nationality, black, Hispanic, and Asian congregations serving people who live in old residential buildings.

A less common alternative has been for the new congregation to borrow large amounts of money, often with the assistance of the denominational mission office, to pay for the construction of the new building. This has been the alternative chosen by hundreds of Caucasian mainline denominational churches with a membership drawn largely from people living in new residential buildings. People living in new homes financed with thirty-year mortgages, working in new offices built with borrowed money, shopping in new retail stores constructed with the use of borrowed money, and sending their children to new schools financed by long-term bonds, often expect to worship God in a new building constructed with borrowed money. This is especially true of the self-identified "evangelical" new churches.

A third alternative has been to meet in rented facilities and avoid the costs of constructing and maintaining a permanent meeting place. The apparent advantages include: (a) no capital investment, (b) lower operating costs, (c) flexibility, (d) intimacy—the limited space forces people to mix with one another, (e) program and ministry rather than care of the building dominate the congregational agenda, and (f) the freedom to move to a new location when appropiate.

This concept has considerable romantic appeal, and scores of congregations have been tempted to try it. (The $900,000 investment by the Reformed Church in America to organize three new congregations in suburban Dallas included the decision to have two landed congregations and one "non-landed" congregation that would rent facilities.) Most of the congregations that chose to avoid owning and operating their own meeting place eventually concluded that the disadvantages outweighed the apparent advantages. The experiences of new congregations choosing to avoid owning and maintaining their own permanent meeting place suggest the following. (1) It is difficult for these congregations to go above one hundred in worship attendance. (2) Newcomers with a substantial investment in that community (such as a $60,000 mortgage on their homes) often are not interested in a congregation that refuses to make an investment in the community. (3) The lack of a highly visible meeting place inhibits the name recognition of the congregation. (4) The absence of a congregationally owned meeting place dominates the agenda and/or seriously influences efforts at long-range planning. (5) The lack of a permanent meeting place often helps to give "a passing parade" character to the membership. (6) The stereotype of the "storefront church" may evoke a negative response from some potential members. (7) It is very difficult to carry on an adequate youth ministry in rented facilities. (8) Congregations in rented or leased facilities often have difficulty providing an appropriate physical setting for corporate worship. (9) Many members appear to be unwilling to make a deep personal investment in a congregation meeting in rented facilities. (10) Few efforts to reach apartment dwellers from a rented meeting place have been effective. (11) In an inflationary era, the decision by one generation not to invest in a building may produce the legacy of a crisis for the next generation of members when the rented facility becomes unavailable or the rental price is increased substantially. (12) Relatively few rental facilities offer adequate storage space. (13) Most important of all, the use of rented facilities ignores the importance and reassurance of "having one's own physical place" in people's lives—one continuing theme in the Old Testament is the search for place.

Before attempting to reinvent that wheel, it might be wiser either (a) to investigate the experiences of congregations using rented facilities in New York, Detroit, Cleveland, Atlanta, Chicago, Dallas, Denver, Albuquerque, San Francisco, and other places, or (b) to go ahead and plan on buying a parcel of land and constructing a new building on it.

Survival Goals or Identity?

To a substantial degree, the launching of a new congregation can be defined in terms of a series of survival goals. These include enlisting sufficient members to create a viable economic unit, finding a temporary meeting place, constructing a permanent building, paying off a large mortgage, and planning to expand the meeting house.

Who are the people who are most comfortable

with these goals? Part of the answer to that question consists of two categories—people born before 1930 and the self-employed. Those two slices of the population carried a disproportionately large share of the new church development of the 1950s and early 1960s.

Gradually, however, they are being replaced in the adult population by people who have a greater interest in identity, self-expression, and personal goals, and who work for someone else. A new generation has come along, and a large share of the clientele for the new churches of the last two decades of this century comes from people who do not share the goals of the people who joined new churches in the 1950s and early 1960s.[10]

What does this mean? In simple terms it means that, if the new church is to be organized around traditional survival goals, it will be most successful if the leaders are drawn from the self-employed and/or people born before 1930. The difficulties with that course of action included: (a) people born before 1930 are disappearing from the scene, not increasing in number, and (b) the number of self-employed men has dropped from 7 million in 1965 to slightly more than 6 million in 1982—while the number of men working for someone else has climbed from less than 40 million to over 50 million in the same period.

Another alternative is to include a disproportionately large number of survival-goal-oriented women in policy making roles. That segment of the population has not been tapped for leadership in proportion to their numbers.

In general, the best lay leadership in the new

153

mission usually comes in a disproportionately large numbers from people who are (a) self-employed, (b) independent entrepreneurs, (c) dependent on their creative gifts to earn a living, and/or (d) are employed in the building trades. The more troublesome lay leadership usually comes in disproportionately large numbers from adults in routine jobs in a large bureaucratic structure who are economically dependent on that bureaucratic structure.

A third alternative is to organize the new mission around identity goals, personal fulfillment, self-expression, and similar goals. The Protestant clergy, however, are just in the beginning stages of developing a new competence with those goals.

Is the Area Already Overchurched?

One of the most common obstacles placed before the proposal to organize a new church is, "This community already is overchurched. The last thing we need here is another church!"

There are approximately a thousand counties in the United States, nearly all of them with a *decreasing* number of residents, where that response may have validity. In another fifteen hundred counties, however, there are two generalizations that should be kept in mind when responding to such statements. First, the larger the number of congregations per one thousand residents, the higher the proportion of churchgoers in the population. While no one has been able to prove the cause-and-effect relationship, the correlation is significant. Second, long-established congregations tend to draw most of the new members from (a) children of members, (b) people who marry a member, and (c) people who already have made a profession of faith and are changing their membership from one chuch to another. By contrast, new missions can be designed so that sixty to eighty percent of the new members are people who previously were not actively related to the life of any worshiping congregation. New churches need not be seen as competition with long-established congregations.

A parallel problem is the desire of many church leaders to gain a "monopoly" in a certain geographical area. This has led to a variety of comity agreements and other arrangements to locate the meeting place of a new congregation at least a mile from any other church building. One result has been construction of new buildings at obscure locations with low visibility that are difficult to find. A better approach is to follow the old rule that the three most important factors in choosing a piece of real estate are (1) location, (2) location, and (3) location. The 1976 study on membership trends by the United Presbyterian Church found that the physical proximity of the church building to other church buildings was not a statistically significant variable in identifying which congregations had an above-average number of accessions to their membership roll. In general, most fishermen prefer to be where the fish are, rather than seek a secluded location. Many department stores have followed a parallel principle in locating a new store in a big shopping mall. There may be a lesson in that in choosing the site for the meeting place of a new congregation.

What Will the Pastor Neglect?

One of the most critical, but also one of the most commonly neglected, issues in church planning comes up about the time the new congregation is ready to begin planning for the first building program.

Up to this point, the mission developer of our hypothetical church has been able to allocate a large amount of time to identifying, visiting, and responding to the needs of potential members. An ever increasing proportion of the minister's time also has been devoted to program development, to planning and conducting worship, to teaching new member classes, to facilitating the transformation from an overgrown small group that functioned rather informally into an organized congregation with the appropriate officers and committee structure, to serving as the pastor to an increasing number of people who seek pastoral care, and to expanding the educational ministry of the new congregation. Everyone agrees that "our pastor is very busy," and the first reaction to that concern will be discussions about the need for a church secretary to come in, at least for three or four mornings a week.

At about this point in the history of the new mission, there is a growing recognition that the time has come to move out of those temporary facilities and to construct their own meeting place. Several of the men have been pushing this very vigorously for some time. Many of the people concerned with the Sunday School or the youth program believe "our own building" is essential if those two ministries are to be able to function adequately. Several members believe the minister is not as aggressive as they desire in pushing the building program. One or two families have left, allegedly because of the delay in going ahead with the new building. Worship attendance is now averaging between 85 and 125 (the typical figure varies among different denominational families), and many believe the congregation will plateau in size without its own building.

A building program will add one more burden on this already busy pastor. What will the minister neglect in order to give time to the building program? Will the pastor cut back on program development? Or enlisting new leaders? Or identifying and recruiting new members? Or will the pastor neglect the pastoral care of the members? Or neglect the pastor's own family? (At this point, it should be noted that new congregations frequently do not offer the family of the mission developer the supportive, nurturing community that often is available to the minister's family in long-established churches.) Or will the pastor try to postpone the time-consuming building program? Or neglect the assimilation of the more recent new members? Or the expansion of the group life, such as the organization of the Bible study groups, or new adult Sunday School classes.

There is no easy or universal solution to this common problem, but the best advice may consist of four suggestions. The minister should (1) concentrate a substantial amount of time on what he or she does best; (2) delegate as much as possible to the laity what they can do and will do most comfortably and most adequately (the most common examples of this are: staffing the building planning committee, the building finance committee, the Christian education committee, and the youth program); (3) not neglect his or her role in new-member enlistment, in leadership development, and in the assimilation of recent new members—these are responsibilities that tend to be neglected by the laity in a new mission; and (4) be able to distinguish between *doing* it and *causing* it to happen—and spend more time on the second leadership role and less time as a shepherd.

These twelves questions do not cover all the issues that will surface during the formulation of a strategy for new church development, but they are some of the questions that come up most often. They can be used in the development or revision of a denominational strategy for church extension.[11] Some of them also apply to the formulation of a denominational strategy for church growth.

5

What Are the Assumptions and Priorities in a Denominational Strategy?

"We're interested in developing a coherent church growth strategy for our denomination in this state. What should we include in the process of formulating such a strategy?"

This question comes up repeatedly, and the best answer is to tailor the strategy to meet the religious needs of the people whom that denomination is seeking to reach, and build on the strengths, assets, and resources of that denomination. In formulating the strategy, there are several questions that should be asked, but only two of them can be discussed here. The first four must be answered from each denomination's particular frame of reference.

1. How does our theological stance and our understanding of our mission shape our strategy?

2. Who are the people we are seeking to reach and serve? What are their unmet religious and personal needs to which we will attempt to respond?

3. How do our traditions, our customs, and our history shape our strategy?

"*Read, mark and inwardly digest*"

— FRANCIS ASBURY

"SOME ASSUMPTIONS BEFORE CONSUMPTION!"

—FRIAR TUCK

4. What are our assets, strengths, resources, and distinctive gifts as a denomination that will serve as the foundation for our strategy?

Those four questions require answers tailored to the particular denomination or regional judicatory. There are, however, two other questions that can be examined in a general context.

What Are Our Assumptions?

Every church growth strategy rests on a set of assumptions. A half dozen that constitute the foundation for this book are discussed in the Introduction. Many of these assumptions tend to be dynamic and to change with the passage of time.[1]

Partly to illustrate the concept, partly to prime the pump, and partly to suggest some assumptions that influence the priorities recommended in the final section of this chapter, it may be useful to list some of these assumptions. All of them are debatable, and several should spark serious discussion.

1. It is assumed that every denominational strategy for church growth will place a high priority on reaching individuals who are not active in the life of any worshiping congregation.

2. It is assumed that the degree of control the denominational leaders have over a specific program will influence their ability to implement that particular facet of the strategy. The crucial issue under this assumption can be stated very brieflly. Who will be in charge? The effective implementation of a denominational church growth strategy,

either nationally or regionally, requires that a full-time staff person be charged with that responsibility. Does your policy make that possible?

3. It is assumed that long-established middle-sized congregations and small churches have a natural tendency to remain on a plateau in size.

4. It is assumed that the smaller the congregation, the greater the changes that will result from the successful implementation of a church growth strategy.

5. It is assumed that every denomination faces limits on the resources it can allocate for a church growth strategy.

6. It is assumed that some form of "cost effectiveness" index will be used to choose among alternative programs and courses of action. The prevalent tendency will be to choose the programs that promise the greatest results for the smallest investment of resources and to minimize those that are high in cost and low in effectiveness.

7. It is assumed that adult male pastors, like most adult males, find it easier to relate to persons above them on the socio-economic scale and more difficult to relate to persons below them on the socio-economic scale. Therefore any male-pastor-centered congregational growth program will tend to produce an upward mobility pattern in that church. This assumption also suggests that those denominations most interested in reaching members of the working class and the new immigrants from other nations may want to rethink their academic requirements for ordination. It may also be wise to consider more women as mission developers in order to expand the outreach to a broader range of people.

162

8. It is assumed that every denomination would prefer to reach and serve a broader range of the total population spectrum than it now includes, and that it is willing to adjust its administrative rules to accommodate that goal. One example of administrative accommodation is the inclination and the ability to "adopt" ethnic, language, racial, or nationality congregations that are seeking a denominational home.

9. It is assumed that every denomination or regional judicatory will want to include several programs in its total strategy and therefore must determine the order of priorities. By definition, it is impossible to have three "number-one priorities." The choice of the number-one priority will be influenced by the assumptions on which that strategy is based as much as by the availability of resources.

10. It is assumed there will be tradeoffs in the development of a denominational strategy. There are some values and some goals that are mutually exclusive. Among the equally repugnant tradeoffs in developing a church strategy are these:

a. Intercongregational cooperation in programming is incompatible with numerical growth.

b. The greater the emphasis on a comprehensive ministry of the laity (including control of the policy making processes), the less likely that congregation will experience numerical growth.

c. The greater the emphasis on participatory democracy in planning and decision making, the greater the probability that congregation will repel the people it is seeking to reach.

d. Short pastorates and numerical growth tend to be incompatible.

e. The "enabler" leadership role for the minister of the congregation with more than three hundred members tends to be incompatible with church growth.

f. Rarely is there gain without pain. Numerical growth usually means change, not simply more of the same.

g. Keeping all the members happy and fostering numerical growth are incompatible goals.

h. The larger the size of the congregation, the greater the dependence on paid staff instead of lay volunteers for implementing a church growth strategy.

i. The faster the pace of numerical growth in the long-established congregation, the greater the chances for the alienation of the pillars who are long-time members.

11. It is assumed that evangelism basically means confronting people with the fact that Jesus Christ is Lord and Savior and inviting them to accept Christ as their personal Savior. By contrast, church growth refers primarily to inviting individuals to unite with a particular congregation. As a result of this distinction, many churches have conducted very effective evangelistic, Christian witness, or missionary programs that resulted in people's making a Christian commitment—and subsequently uniting with some other congregation. This experience has been very common among hundreds of inner-city churches. Therefore, an effective denominational strategy will include *both* an evangelistic dimension *and* a process for encouraging people to unite with churches of that denominational family, including people who had made a profession of faith much earlier. An effective church

growth strategy also will be designed to reach those who have never made a Christian commitment, the "dropouts," and also the long-time committed Christians who are moving to a new place of residence.

12. Finally, it is assumed that congregational leaders will find it beneficial to secure the perspective of outside "third-party" observers. Therefore, a denominational strategy should include provisions for enlisting and training people who can serve directly in this third-party role with congregations. (This contrasts with the approach that trains a cadre of people who in turn train congregational leaders to work in their own churches, but does not include provision for the direct intervention of third parties in congregational life.)

What are the assumptions on which the church growth strategy for your denominaton is based? How do they compare with the assumptions listed above?

What Are Our Priorities?

Within the context of these assumptions, it is possible to suggest a set of priorities for a denominational strategy for church growth. There are ten components to this strategy, and they are presented with the highest priority first and the lowest priority last.

The first priority in any denominational strategy should be on organizing new congregations. There are several reasons behind this recommendation. First, the organization of new congregations is the most effective single method of reaching people without any active church affiliation. Second, as a group, newly organized congregations have a more rapid rate of growth than any other type church. Third, in the organization of new congregations, denominational leaders have a greater degree of control over what happens than in any other component of a denominational church growth strategy. This is a strategy that can be implemented with a minimum degree of cooperation from other parties. Fourth, if a systematic effort is made, a strong emphasis on new church development can enable a denomination to broaden its outreach to reach and serve people it is not likely to touch through existing congregations. Finally, those denominations that are experiencing an increase in the number of congregations are also registering numerical growth, while those that are experiencing a decrease in the number of congregations are experiencing a decrease in the number of members.

There are at least three dimensions to this issue of new congregations as a source of denominational growth. One is the organization of new, predominant black, Anglo, or Native American churches. The second (and perhaps this should be the first) priority is the organization of new congregations to serve the new immigration into the United States. The third is to "adopt" black, Hispanic, Asian, and other already established minority congregations who are seeking a denominational home.

The second priority in a denominational strategy should be to encourage the numerical growth of large churches. There are six reasons behind this recommendation. First, this is the second most effective means for a denomination to reach more people.[2] Second, if given a choice, a disproportionately large number of the churchgoers born after 1945 are choosing large churches. Third, in many churches the denominational leaders have considerable influence, not only in the choice of a senior minister, but also in the number and area of specialization of program staff members—and these are often critical factors in the growth of large congregations. Fourth, the denominational leaders frequently have considerable influence in the planning and decision-making processes of large churches. Fifth, in order to remain on a plateau in size, the typical thousand-member congregation has to receive an average of two new members every week. This usually means that the large church has considerable experience in identifying, attracting, and receiving new members. From a purely pragmatic point of view, it usually is easier to help a congregation expand an ongoing new-member-enlistment system than it is for a small congregation on a plateau to launch a new church growth effort. Finally, the larger the congregation, the less disruptive are the changes that accompany numerical expansion. Since there is a natural human resistance to change, it is easier and less disruptive for the large churches to expand substantially than it is for small congregations.

The third component of a denominational church growth strategy—and some might rank this higher—would be to develop a program designed to help congregations improve their ability to assimilate new members. In thousands of congregations, nearly as many members drop into inactivity out the "back door" as come into the congregation via the "front door."[3] This is an especially serious concern in large churches. The critical

element of such a component of the denominational strategy would be to train pastors and lay
volunteers in developing a systematic caring
program.[4]

The fourth component could be a program to
train pastors moving into "single-cell" small congregations in the strategy for growth described in
the first chapter of this book. The fifth priority
would be to encourage longer pastorates. While
there is no evidence that long pastorates automatically result in numerical growth, it is rare to find a
congregation that has experienced a long period of
sustained growth without the benefit of a long
pastorate.

The sixth component would be directed at
middle-sized congregations that have been on a
plateau in size for several years. Several suggestions
for such a strategy can be found in the second
chapter. A valuable and productive element of this
program could be for each regional judicatory to
enlist and train a cadre of lay volunteers who would
serve as outside "third-party auditors." On an
unscheduled and unannounced basis, these trained
lay volunteers would visit churches and identify the
assets and strengths of the parish as perceived
through the eyes of a first-time visitor, and also
point out the barriers to an effective outreach.[5] This
could be part of a comprehensive effort to train lay
volunteers in church growth concepts.

The seventh part of a denominational strategy
could be to change the reporting system—especially the annual reports from congregations to
denominational headquarters—to encourage congregations to set goals in new-member enlistment
and to hold themselves accountable for the attain-

ment of these goals. Such a change in the reporting system would also encourage the regional judicatories to develop a support system for these goals in evangelism.[6] The reporting system does influence congregational priorities, and it can be designed to make evangelism and church growth a high priority for both congregations and regional judicatories.

The eighth part of a denominational strategy would be to encourage the various auxiliary organizations in congregations to see themselves as agents of church growth. This would include the women's organization,[7] the men's fellowship, the youth group, the choir, and the adult Sunday school classes. It would also include the program committees, such as worship, music, social ministries, education, and missions. Prospective members could be encouraged to serve on these committees. This could expand the perspective and enrich the program of these committees, and also offer a new entry point for potential new members into that congregation.

The ninth priority would be to help congregations attain the skills necessary for reactivating their inactive members. There are two reasons for ranking this as the ninth priority. First, there are only ten items on this list. If there were twenty suggestions for a denominational strategy on this list, a program to reactivate inactive members would be nineteenth on the list. Second, in most cases this turns out to be a high-investment program (in terms of time and energy) that has frustration as its major outcome. The vast majority of the inactive church members who return to an active role do so after uniting with a different congregation.

The tenth and lowest priority in a denominational

strategy should be to help those congregations that once were neighborhood churches reestablish themselves as geographical parishes. During the past three decades, tens of millions of dollars and immeasurable quantities of time and energy have been devoted to this goal. The three major results of these efforts have been guilt, frustration, and despair. "Every church should serve its community," was based on a naïve and primarily rural definition of *community* that was not consistent with either the biblical or historical definition of that word.[8] The concept of an urban church that serves a geographical parish, in which the members live near that meeting place and "neighbor" with one another, applies most appropriately to: (a) the *first* residents of a large subdivision or *new* housing, (b) the 1920s and earlier decades, (c) a tiny number of elite congregations, (d) a highly authoritarian social system in which an elite leadership group is able and willing to suppress the desires of the members to exercise a freedom of choice, and (e) the early days in the formation of a few congregations designed to serve a group of recently arrived immigrants from another part of the world.

How do these suggested components of a denominational strategy match the content of the church growth program for your denomination? Are your priorities consistent with the assumptions and the goals of your strategy? Who reviews that relationship between assumptions, values, and goals on the one hand and the priorities among the various components in your denominational strategy on the other?

In conclusion, it is important to remember the value of tailoring the strategy to fit the local context.

This is a book of suggestions, not prescriptions. It does not matter whether the focus is on developing a comprehensive denominational church growth strategy, on helping the small single-cell congregation become a multi-cell church, on planning for the growth of middle-sized or large parishes, or on starting new missions. The strategy should reflect the resources, the distinctive characteristics, the potentials, and the unique role of that part of the body of Christ.

NOTES

Introduction

1. For an elaboration of this argument, see Lyle E. Schaller, *Activating the Passive Church* (Nashville: Abingdon Press, 1981), pp. 5-28; and Lyle E. Schaller, *The Small Church Is Different!* (Nashville: Abingdon Press, 1982), chap. 1.

2. For the origin of this delightfully apt phrase, see Reginald W. Bibley and Merlin B. Brinkerhoff, "The Circulation of the Saints: A Study of People Who Join Conservative Churches," *Journal for the Scientific Study of Religion,* vol. 12, 1973, pp. 173-83. They found two percent of the new members of the twenty evangelical churches studied had not had any previous church affiliation, and the vast majority had come from some other evangelical congregation.

3. For an extensive review of some of the distinctive characteristics of adult new members, see Lyle E. Schaller, "New Members: Old Members," *Church Growth: America* (January-February, 1980).

Chapter 1

1. For an elaboration of this response, see Carl S. Dudley, *Making the Small Church Effective* (Nashville: Abingdon Press, 1978), pp. 55-59. An excellent booklet on this subject is Wesley C. Boles, *The Vital Signs: Evangelism in Small Congregations* (New York: United Presbyterian Church in the U.S.A., 1978).

2. Warren Hartman of the Board of Discipleship of the United Methodist Church and Carl Dudley on the faculty at McCormick Presbyterian Seminary in Chicago have both written extensively on the tendency of small-membership churches to remain on a plateau in size.

3. Dudley, *Making the Small Church Effective,* pp. 32-35.

4. For an elaboration of this and other concepts in the process of

planned change *from within an organization,* see Lyle E. Schaller, *The Change Agent* (Nashville: Abingdon Press, 1972).

Chapter 2

1. For a classification system based on worship attendance, see Lyle E. Schaller, *The Multiple Staff and the Larger Church* (Nashville: Abingdon Press, 1980), pp. 27-35.

2. Diagnostic and prescriptive comments on that issue can be found in Lyle E. Schaller, *Activating the Passive Church* (Nashville: Abingdon Press 1981).

Chapter 3

1. The leadership style of the minister will vary according to personality, gifts, experience, and the church's polity, but an effective church growth strategy requires the senior minister to function as an active, aggressive, and initiating leader.

2. For a discussion of the difference between the dynamics of large groups and small groups, see Lyle E. Schaller, *Effective Church Planning* (Nashville: Abingdon Press, 1979), pp. 17-63.

3. Other variables in staffing the large church are discussed in Lyle E. Schaller, *The Multiple Staff and the Larger Church* (Nashville: Abingdon Press, 1980), pp. 51-84.

4. For a statement on the importance of music in the large church see Lyle E. Schaller, "Music in the Large Church," *Choristers Guild Letters,* (March, 1980).

5. A very useful kit for developing a systematic approach to the care of members is L. Ray Sells and Donald LaSuer, *The Caring System* (Pasadena, Calif.; Christian Communications, 1979).

Chapter 4

1. For a critical review of comity agreements, see Lyle E. Schaller, *Planning for Protestantism in Urban America* (Nashville: Abingdon Press, 1965), pp. 98-117.

2. For a more extensive discussion of the importance of physical place in people's lives, see Lyle E. Schaller, *Effective Church Planning* (Nashville: Abingdon Press, 1979), pp. 65-92.

3. For a very instructive statement on this issue, see Ezra Earl Jones, *Strategies for New Churches* (New York: Harper & Row, 1976), pp. 108-18.

4. For a useful introduction to this basic concept, see Eugene Lewis, *Public Entrepreneurship: Toward a Theory of Bureaucratic Political Power* (Bloomington, Indiana: Indiana University Press, 1980). See also the influence of achievement and the willingness to take risks, as

NOTES

described by David McClelland, *The Achieving Society* (New York: Van Nostrand, 1961).

5. James MacGregor Burns, *Leadership* (New York: Harper & Row, 1978), pp. 4, 257-397.

6. Milton and Rose Friedman, *Free to Choose* (New York: Avon Books, 1980), pp. 165-72.

7. While it is a peripheral issue, it should be noted that in several predominantly Anglo denominations seeking to reach and serve ethnic minorities, the issue of financial subsidies for new ministries has become the focal point for the struggle over power. Sometimes that struggle obscures the initial purpose of the financial subsidies.

8. For a thorough definition of, and apologetic for, the homogeneous unit principles, see C. Peter Wagner, *Our Kind of People* (Atlanta: John Knox Press, 1979), and C. Peter Wagner, *Church Growth and the Whole Gospel* (New York: Harper & Row, 1981), pp. 166-81.

9. For an extensive discussion of the value of redefining role at the appropriate time, see Lyle E. Schaller, *Activating the Passive Church* (Nashville: Abingdon Press, 1981), pp. 71-99.

10. For a more extended analysis of this distinction, see Lyle E. Schaller, *Understanding Tomorrow* (Nashville: Abingdon Press, 1976), pp. 32-37; Joseph Veroff, Elizabeth Douvan, and Richard A. Kulka, *The Inner American* (New York: Basic Books, 1981); and Daniel Yankelovich, *New Rules* (New York: Random House, 1981).

11. Several denominations have prepared resources to help in the formulation of a strategy for planting new congregations. An excellent example is the "New Church Resources" notebook published by the Division of Evangelism and Church Extension of the United Church Board for Homeland Ministries. An order form for that and other evangelism resources can be secured by writing Church Leadership Resources, 1400 North Seventh Street, St. Louis, Missouri 63105. Please enclose a stamped and addressed return envelope.

Chapter 5

1. For a fascinating overview of some of the characteristics, assumptions, and values on contemporary denominational church growth strategies see Alfred C. Krass, "What the Mainline Denominations Are Doing in Evangelism," *The Christian Century* (May 2, 1979), pp. 490-96.

2. For an interesting statistical analysis of this tendency for new missions and large congregations to account for most of the new growth in a regional judicatory, see J. L. Thomas, "Evangelism and New Mission Churches," a paper presented to the Executive Board Staff of the Baptist General Conference of Texas, February 1976.

3. For suggestions on this, see Lyle E. Schaller, *Assimilating New Members* (Nashville: Abingdon Press, 1978).

175

NOTES

4.   An excellent tool for this is L. Ray Sells and Donald LaSuer, *The Caring System* (Pasadena, California: Christian Communication, 1979).

5.   For an excellent description of one such program, see Walter A. Fortrey, "Secret Agents of Worship," *The Lutheran* (February 3, 1982), pp. 12-14.

6.   For an elaboration of this concept, see Lyle E. Schaller, "Apportionment for Evangelism," *Circuit Rider* (May 1981).

7.   For a few suggestions on this concept, see Lyle E. Schaller, "Can the Women's Organization Be an Instrument of Church Growth?" *Church Growth: America* (March-April 1979).

8.   For an excellent statement on the concept of community as a social network, rather than as a geographical place, see Thomas Bender, *Community and Social Change in America* (New Brunswick, N.Y.: Rutgers University Press, 1978).